For Real?

Christ's Presence in the Eucharist

DEACON DENNIS LAMBERT

Liguori

PRAISE FOR *FOR REAL? CHRIST'S PRESENCE IN THE EUCHARIST*

The Holy Eucharist is not only the "source and summit" of the Catholic faith, it is quite possibly the most misunderstood mystery within Catholicism. What a tremendous gift this book is for souls longing for our Lord and answers. Deacon Dennis Lambert methodically explains not only *what* we believe as Catholics but, even more importantly, *why* we believe it. Drawing on trusted biblical scholars and the timeless wisdom of the saints, the reader is given a simple yet profound understanding of the Eucharist as God's greatest gift and his plan of salvation. With relatable stories and Scripture verses, *For Real? Christ's Presence in the Eucharist* is a must for Catholics who want to dive deeper into the sacramental mystery and learn how to help those they love do the same.

Mark Hart, CIO, Life Teen International,
Catholic author, speaker, co-host of *The Catholic Guy Show*
on SiriusXM's the Catholic Channel

A thoughtful explanation of Christ's Real Presence in the Eucharist that is approachable and readable without compromising the depth or history of the "source and summit" of our faith. I highly recommend everyone read this book and fall in love once again with Jesus, who never leaves us and is truly present at every Mass.

Ryan Hanning, PhD,
author and adjunct professor, University of Mary;
fellow, the Institute for Catholic Theology

Deacon Dennis Lambert describes himself as a "Thomas" who wants to know the why behind everything. If you are a skeptic, cynic, or doubter, this book is for you. You will never look at the Eucharist, read certain Scripture passages, or even see the Catholic Church the same way once the pieces come together. Because of this book, you'll be able to share the Eucharist with others. Welcome to the relay race!

Deacon Pedro Guevara-Mann,
producer and host of the *Salt and Light Hour*
on SiriusXM's the Catholic Channel

For Real? Christ's Presence in the Eucharist makes a profound-but-challenging topic approachable for everyday Catholics. Without sacrificing any of the great mystery, Deacon Dennis provides explanations and historical background that beautifully illustrate the Church's understanding of the Eucharist and how to communicate this great truth to others. This book will be a blessing for teachers and students of the faith!

Steve Greene,
director, Kino Catechetical Institute
and co-host of the podcast *The Catholic Conversation*

With wonderful clarity, *For Real? Christ's Presence in the Eucharist* addresses one of the most important subjects of our times. Using a relay-race analogy, Deacon Dennis Lambert lays out how the message of the Real Presence of Christ in the Eucharist began with Jesus himself and was passed, unchanged, to the Church of today. It was even prefigured in many passages in the Old Testament. I wholeheartedly recommend this book to all who seek to draw closer to our Lord and Savior.

Deacon Bob Evans,
Diocese of Phoenix's assistant director of deacon personnel,
author of *Walking the Parables of Jesus*

Imprimi Potest: Stephen T. Rehrauer, CSsR, Provincial
Denver Province, the Redemptorists

Imprimatur: "In accordance with CIC 827, permission to publish has been granted
on December 13, 2021, by the Most Reverend Mark S. Rivituso, Auxiliary Bishop,
Archdiocese of St. Louis. Permission to publish is an indication that nothing
contrary to Church teaching is contained in this work. It does not imply any
endorsement of the opinions expressed in the publication; nor is any liability
assumed by this permission."

Published by Liguori Publications, Liguori, Missouri 63057

Liguori Publications, a nonprofit corporation, is an apostolate of the
Redemptorists (Redemptorists.com).

To order this book, visit Liguori.org or call 800-325-9521.

For Real? Christ's Presence in the Eucharist

ISBN 978-0-7648-2853-9

Cataloging-in-Publication data is on file with the Library of Congress

Cover design: Wendy Barnes
Cover image: Sebastian Duda / Shutterstock

Printed in the United States of America
26 25 24 23 22 / 5 4 3 2 1
First Edition

Contents

To my wife, Debbie:
You are a gift. I could not have asked for a better
companion to help navigate our mutual pursuit of heaven.

Preface

This book is a work of apologetics for the Real Presence of Christ Jesus in the Eucharist. It aims to provide an intellectual case to support the Catholic Church's teaching about the Eucharist as absolute truth.

This is vital for two reasons. The first is that credible research has found that more than one-third of all Catholics who attend Mass regularly—at least once a week—believe the Eucharist is just a symbol. A 2019 Pew Research study shows 37 percent of these Catholics "don't believe that the Communion bread and wine actually become the Body and Blood of Christ." These individuals join the Protestant/Evangelical faithful, who largely believe that holy Communion is merely a symbol or remembrance of the Last Supper. The study also shows there is a lack of understanding on transubstantiation and about it being held as a firm position of Church teaching.

The second reason relates to the first: if what the Church teaches regarding the Eucharist is true—that Christ makes himself substantially present every day, at every Mass—it would likely become a game changer for all who call themselves Christian.

I believe making this rational, logical case for the Eucharist is imperative because those who don't currently believe in the Real Presence have likely not been offered enough information to dissuade their lack of understanding and in turn shift their belief. I should know since I once identified as a nonbeliever in the Real Presence. However, that changed when I began my own objective research into the topic.

While there are many books written in defense of the Eucharist, most have a singular focus, like: What did Jesus, his apostles, and the Church Fathers teach about the Eucharist? What prefigurements (foreshadowing) from the Old Testament hinted at, or pointed to, the Eucharist?

Like that of a skilled tailor, my goal is to seamlessly weave all these topics together in a single narrative by using the imagery of a relay race. The book's basic premise is that eucharistic teaching begins with Jesus at the starting line (leg one of the race). Leg one is by far the most important and convincing component. If you are currently a nonbeliever or skeptic about the Real Presence, my guess is that this section, at a minimum, will trigger thoughts within you. I hope that skeptics and nonbelievers will find it transformative. In this relay analogy, Jesus flawlessly hands his teachings to those who followed right after him, the apostles for leg two. After examining the apostles' teachings and beliefs, the "baton"—and our study— is handed cleanly to the next teachers of the faith, the early Church Fathers for leg three. From there, that baton of belief and teaching is handed to the present-day Church in leg four, the final leg we still run today.

Contrary to the belief of some, the Eucharist is not theology that was created by the Catholic Church hundreds of years after Jesus' time on earth. This teaching began with Jesus and has remained unaltered.

I believe three groups will likely benefit from reading this book. The first comprises Catholics and non-Catholics who do not believe that the Eucharist contains the full person, full humanity, and complete divinity of our Lord Jesus Christ. The second group includes Catholics who are unsure about this truth, which Pew says totals about 5 percent. These people may be inclined to believe, but their rational minds cannot jump the last hurdle to total belief. The third group includes those who already believe in Christ's Real Presence in the Eucharist. If you don't believe in or are indifferent to Christ's Real Presence in the Eucharist, consider:

- If you came across convincing evidence that our Lord was indeed fully present in the Eucharist, would it have a positive and substantial effect on your faith journey and practice?
- To this point in your life, have you taken the time to hear or study the Catholic evidence for the Eucharist?

If the answers are yes to the first question and no to the second, do yourself a favor and keep reading. The worst thing that can happen is you will have spent a few hours learning what the Catholic Church teaches about the Eucharist. At best, this book can draw you closer to God and improve your life.

If you already believe, keep reading. Learning more about the rational arguments for what you already believe in your heart to be true can help equip you to give a reasoned response to those who question your belief and the topic as a whole. This book likely will deepen and strengthen your own faith life and belief in the Eucharist.

I can think of few other topics that are more deserving of an honest and intellectual investigation. No matter where you are on the spectrum of belief in the Real Presence, I hope you are intrigued enough to forge ahead. Remember, I was once an unbeliever and skeptic. It took rational soul-searching for me to realize that Christ presents himself as a total gift to us within his personal gift of the Eucharist.

CHAPTER 1

The Thomas in Me

When God gave people the cognitive process, I think he made two kinds. We either identify with Thomas or we are childlike innocents.

To understand what it means to be a "Thomas," we turn to Thomas the Apostle. Recall how Thomas, having been absent when the resurrected Jesus first appeared to his apostles, refused to believe that Jesus rose from the dead until he could put his fingers into the wound in Jesus' side. Also remember how, in John 14, Jesus told his apostles he was going to prepare a place for them in heaven. Then Jesus added that where he was going, they knew the way. Thomas, needing clarity, responds, "Master, we do not know where you are going; how can we know the way?" (John 14:5).

Like the apostle, skeptical "Thomases" of today want to know the why behind everything. They require thorough explanations and rational, logical answers for all their questions before solidifying their beliefs.

Conversely, the childlike innocents typically need little to no explanation, logic, or knowledge to understand and believe complex matters, most especially substances of faith. They are guided by something—most often identified as "the heart"—that not only defies logic but often triumphs over it. When it comes to receiving faith, Jesus often draws upon the image of a child. One of the best examples comes from the Gospel of Matthew. The disciples ask:

"Who is the greatest in the kingdom of heaven?" [Jesus] called a child over, placed it in their midst, and said, "Amen, I say to you, unless you turn and become like children, you will not enter the kingdom of heaven. Whoever humbles himself like this child is the greatest in the kingdom of heaven. And whoever receives one child such as this in my name receives me."

Matthew 18:1–5

Jesus holds up the image of the child not just because of the little one's inherent innocence but because of the child's dependency and unflinching confidence in his parents. When young children see a parent at a distance, crouched down, arms held wide open, they don't stop to analyze what they're seeing. They sprint toward those extended arms until they are engulfed in an embrace of love.

And so it is with us and our faith. God calls us to come to him as a trusting child. Still, he created me with a Thomas disposition. I don't know why. I tried earlier in my life to be controlled by the heart, but my ever-probing mind always found a way to take the lead. I was, and still greatly am, a Thomas. If you can relate, I need not elaborate on the complexities involved when we approach the topic of the Eucharist.

God gave us rational, high-functioning minds for a reason. While we need to use the treasure of our minds, it should always be in coordination with another superior gift God gave us—our hearts. I remember how the importance of maintaining this balance was eventually grafted into me. It occurred when, as a young man, I read:

> Reason is in fact the path to faith, and faith takes over when reason can say no more.
> *The Ascent to Truth,* Thomas Merton

God gave us a heart, a mind, faith, and reason to use in partnership. Real problems of faith can occur when we weigh in only on the side of the intellect. To illustrate this, here's a quintessential Thomas moment from my life.

LEARNING FROM MY MISTAKES

I was a cradle Catholic whose "cradle" was insulated with love and devotion to the faith. My family went to Mass every Sunday and on every holy day of obligation. Like many Catholics then and today, the Lamberts had a preferred pew. Ours was in the center section, the second pew from the altar. I can still recall my dad's tendency to lean forward and go back every three seconds. I am convinced he was unaware of this habit or of me mimicking it.

I loved and looked up to both of my parents, especially for their unwavering sense of service, evident in their continual willingness to help others. They were both very involved in the parish and would often invite the sisters who ran the church's school, along with the priests, to our home whenever we had a significant gathering. It was in that grade school and church—St. Joseph's in Round Lake, Illinois—that my siblings and I received our grammar school education and celebrated the sacraments. A generation later, my own two children followed suit, attending the same grade school and receiving the sacraments in the same parish church.

My Catholic education continued at Carmel High School in Mundelein, Illinois. There, two life-changing events occurred during my junior year. The first was meeting my future wife, Debbie. The second involved me taking an initial, deep, interest in my faith. I would like to be able to say this interest sprang from an inward Christlike awakening, but in reality, almost all of my motivation was fueled by intellectual curiosity inspired by the teaching of a Carmelite priest named Fr. Tom Drolet. I found his religion classes fascinating and couldn't get enough. His method of teaching Scripture and theology was rational and relatable. Who wrote what Gospel and when? Who was the audience for each Gospel? How does Judaism connect with Christianity?

From that point on, I was hooked on the academics of Christianity. I still fondly recall Fr. Tom's enthusiasm in explaining what "brood of vipers" meant in context to the contempt Jesus had for the Pharisees. Imagine my excitement when I learned that Fr. Tom would also be teaching religion my senior year.

During my first few years of college, I began to develop many questions about my Catholic faith, which led to all sorts of problems, including internal conflicts. The questions became so numerous and contentious that I began to wonder why I still professed to be a Catholic. At this crossroads, I made a crucial error.

Also during this time, I began taking bass guitar lessons from a fellow named Bill, who was a few years older than me. I eventually accepted Bill's invitation to play softball on his nondenominational evangelical church team. As I got to know my teammates, I saw a goodness in them. And, unlike most Catholics I had known, they were genuinely willing to talk about faith and the Bible, which appealed to me.

So rather than going to a priest with my mounting questions of faith, I went to these men and their families, to their Bible studies, and to individual meetings with their pastor. Of course, they had answers to my questions. I found this small evangelical community to be staunchly anti-Catholic and eager to have a chance to save me from the clutches of what they perceived to be an evil institution. Even more impressive to me at the time was how they used Scripture to back up all of their answers.

Like the parable of the sower of seeds, initially I sprang up like the heartiest of plants. I had seemingly not only found answers to my questions, but also real, authentic faith! Thankfully, in this instance, I was like the seed thrown on rocky ground and those evangelical roots did not take. After two years, I came to discover numerous ambiguities and flaws in their answers and assertions.

Two years after my subtle schism with the Church, I scheduled a meeting with a priest at my parish to discuss my long-held questions and "problems" with the Church. As grace would have it, the priest I was slated to meet with was a new associate pastor for my parish. His name? Fr. Tom Drolet!

I walked out of that session feeling like a giant. Having received the grace of the sacrament of confession certainly played a big part in that feeling, but having my questions answered with such depth, logic, and love undoubtedly contributed as well. I learned that if you have questions about your Catholic faith, first talk to a Catholic source. About two years after that meeting, Fr. Tom Drolet witnessed Debbie and I celebrate the sacrament of matrimony.

I remember my first Mass after two years of separation. It was a Sunday. As I passed through St. Joseph's Church, there in the second row center sat my parents. The walk down the aisle was surreal. I was home. But there was one more emotional, familial pardon that I needed to receive to solidify my return. I quietly entered the pew behind my parents, leaned over, placed a hand on my dad's shoulder and whispered in his ear, "I'm back." He turned slowly, put his hand on mine, and said, "I was just praying, at this very moment, for you to return to the Church" (insert tears of joy here).

As I look back, I understand that my evangelical friends had the best of intentions. They taught me things that are still important to my faith today, namely love for the Bible and the importance of having a personal relationship with Christ.

Suffice it to say that my two-year detour served me well, most especially when I have occasion to interact with or minister to any of our Protestant brothers and sisters.

Still, the experience outside the Church had residual negative effects on me that lasted several years. Even though I was—with great excitement—back in the Church, I found many of the hard-line, evangelical, anti-Catholic positions I'd gathered in my absence difficult to shed. The importance and reverence due our Blessed Mother was one of them, and that's something for which I continually ask forgiveness. The other was clinging to the Protestant view of the symbolic nature of the Eucharist. In fact, the thing that most strongly propelled me to write this book was the discovery of my children's Communion banners.

As I said, my children attended the same Catholic grade school I did. At three years apart in age, they shared about the same practices in preparing to celebrate their first Communion. Part of the catechesis at this time involved parental participation in creating a Communion banner. The family determined the content, with the only stipulation being that it relate to the sacrament of holy Communion. These banners were placed on the outside of the pew during the Communion Mass, thereby reserving that pew for each new communicant's family.

It was presumed that the parents would talk with their child about the meaning and purpose of the sacrament. While my wife took the lead on the banner's art, I oversaw the language and the subsequent sacramental conversation with our kids. Both of my children's banners contained the same two words, my creation: "I Remember."

On the surface, there isn't anything wrong with remembering the passion of our Lord, beginning with the Last Supper, but those words, my words, were intentional—they focused on the memory, because that was the extent of my belief surrounding the Eucharist. We gave zero time to putting in childlike terms anything about Christ's Real Presence in the Eucharist. I purposely held back from my sweet, beautiful, innocent children that when they receive their first holy Communion, and every time after, they would receive a physical part of our Saving Lord. Also absent was any explanation of the profound grace they would be receiving. For me, at that time, Communion was a *symbol* of a greater reality and not a greater reality unto itself.

I stumbled on those banners about a year ago in a dresser drawer. I remember clutching them in my hands, one navy blue, the other teal, and crying. I could not believe what I had done. With much thanks, and by God's grace, somewhere during my spiritual journey I began reading the likes of Catholic apologist Scott Hahn. These writings instilled within me a herculean desire to understand more fully the mystery of the Eucharist. And, thanks be to God, my understanding of the Eucharist indeed changed. To say that I fully understand and accept all the teaching of the Church regarding it would be an understatement. Like a redeemed Thomas, I kneel before his Real Presence in the Eucharist and declare, "My Lord and my God!"

I AM NOT ALONE

In my search for a fuller understanding of this most revered sacrament, it did not take me long to realize there were other Catholics whose views on the Eucharist differed from the teachings of Christ and his Church. This is exemplified in the Pew study discussed earlier. This reality only solidified my desire to write this book.

I began my personal deep dive into the topic of the Eucharist as a scathed and misinformed skeptic, but through prayer, study, and grace, I have emerged as a full-throated believer in and evangelist for the Eucharist. To further emphasize the importance of this topic for Catholics and non-Catholics alike, allow me to paraphrase a story Fr. Michael Schmitz tells on his CD *True Worship*.

Imagine you knew for certain that Jesus was going to make an in-person appearance tomorrow at noon at a park near you. By "for certain," I mean the information had been vetted extensively. Every news outlet was offering nonstop coverage, and the major national television networks planned to broadcast the event live. Would you go see for yourself?

Fr. Mike ventures most of us would go to the park. To see Jesus...to be in his presence...who wouldn't? Fr. Mike goes on to make a most salient point. "This is exactly what is going on every day in every Catholic church on earth," he says. "Christ makes himself fully and completely present to us, in the Eucharist." Does the prospect that God reveals himself to us in a real way place within you the desire to investigate the idea of Real Presence more fully? Is anything more worthy of examination than the possibility that heaven kisses earth at every Mass?

I've learned that conveying the truth of the Real Presence of the Eucharist is not a matter of winning an academic argument. Rather, it is about the grace and transformative power that comes from understanding and embracing the eucharistic truth. This acceptance should also serve as the stimulus that drives all the faithful to promulgate its reality.

But how? Certainly it's difficult trying to explain what is by definition a mystery to a world filled with prove-it-to-me, Thomaslike cynics. The most knowledgeable among us may have little problems explaining it. But after accepting this truth, how can people like you and I provide a compelling explanation to others? This speaks to the twofold purpose of this book: First, present information that can radically change, affirm, or deepen one's belief in the Real Presence of Christ in the Eucharist. Second, deliver a succinct, easy-to-remember, and thought-provoking way to share this truth with others. I hope the image of a relay race will help the latter.

RELAY-RACE METAPHOR

I chose the relay-race metaphor because of its two memorable features: the continuum of a relay race and the four parts of the race. A relay race has four legs, with each one continuing the previous leg, all of which form one race. In a relay race, the baton must be passed from one runner to the next. If the baton is passed successfully and never dropped, the race is unified and its results are valid. Thus the race can't be viewed as four separate races but rather as one continuous race.

To explain the Real Presence of Christ in the Eucharist, I am employing the metaphor of a four-leg relay race, with the teaching of the Real Presence as the "baton." This helps the reader understand the truth of this teaching and pass it on. The components comprise:

Leg one, the Teachings of Jesus Himself
Leg two, the Teachings of the Apostles
Leg three, the Teachings of the Early Church Fathers
Leg four, the Teachings of the Church Today

In this relay analogy, the teaching of the Real Presence of Christ in the Eucharist starts with Jesus himself. He "runs" (teaches) the first leg before handing the baton (Real Presence teaching) of this transformative reality to his apostles, who spread the Good News before a handoff to the early Church Fathers, who make the Real Presence known before passing the baton to the leaders and Church of today. Throughout, the baton never drops; the teachings have never changed from the time of Jesus himself.

Some have suggested that our Catholic view of the Eucharist, specifically the Real Presence, was a theology created sometime long after Jesus, perhaps by hundreds of years. But as we discuss each leg of the relay, it will become unmistakably clear that this teaching started with Jesus, as recorded in the Bible, and that it remains fully intact and unchanged to this day.

The many prefigurements to the Real Presence found in the Old Testament offer additional support to the amazing continuation on this teaching of Jesus. The potent combination of the guidance of our Lord and the eucharistic foreshadowing leave little room for doubt about the validity of this most precious, sacred, and life-giving reality. These prefigurements will be discussed in the pages ahead.

CHAPTER 2

Eucharist Refresher

Before sprinting fully into our relay metaphor, a refresher course on other faith essentials that are so richly connected to our understanding of the Eucharist is appropriate. Look on this review as the "starting blocks" that the first runners use in a relay race. A grounded, steady foundation fosters a greater hope of success.

Following a review of these cornerstones of Catholic belief, I'll clarify some potentially confusing misunderstandings about the Eucharist. This chapter concludes with a compare-and-contrast of the Catholic views of holy Communion versus those held by Protestants.

KEY EUCHARIST-RELATED TERMS: SACRAMENTS AND GRACE

Because the Eucharist is not simply one of the seven sacraments of the Church but the "source and summit" of the Catholic faith, it is important to define terms. The *Baltimore Catechism* offers a succinct, yet profoundly stated, twelve-word definition that reveals the essence of a sacrament:

> A sacrament is an outward sign, instituted by Christ to give grace.

This easy-to-remember definition says there are three parts in every sacrament: an outward sign...instituted by Christ... gives grace. Here's a look at each component.

Outward Sign and Inward Reality

We are attracted and drawn into what we can observe. We respond to and navigate our way through our environment by way of our five senses: touch, sight, hearing, taste, and smell. We are tactile beings who depend on our senses to interpret the world around us. Understanding this, God designed our sacraments to have observable components, commonly referred to as "outward signs" and/or symbols. At a baptism we can see the outward sign of water being poured on a baby's head. We hear the external signs in the spoken words of the priest or deacon: "I baptize you in the name of the Father, and of the Son, and of the Holy Spirit."

During the consecration of the Mass, we see the outward sign of the sacrament of holy Communion as the priest elevates the bread. Our ears hear his words, "This is my body." As we hear those words and see the raised host, we are physically drawn to these observable signs.

But we are not just drawn into sensory matter. These observable actions serve also as literal signs that point to something deeper than what is picked up by our senses. They orient us toward an invisible reality, an unseen act of God's grace. Saint Augustine eloquently intertwines these dimensions of the observable and the unseen acts of God when he describes sacraments as "the visible sign of an invisible grace."

While our eyes see and our ears hear, within the sacraments we find our hearts responding to something deeper, more pervasive, and lasting. In the example of the Eucharist, heaven has just kissed earth. Christ himself has just become substantially present to us on his holy altar!

One of the most resonating explanations of a sacrament having both a tangible and unseen reality comes from the US Conference of Catholic Bishops (USCCB). Within the bishops' teaching on sacraments and sacramentals, they write: "We recognize that the sacraments have a visible and invisible reality, a reality open to all the human senses but grasped in its God-given depths with the eyes of faith. When parents hug their children, for example, the visible reality we see is the hug. The invisible reality the hug conveys is love. We cannot 'see' the love the hug expresses, though sometimes we can see its nurturing effect in the child."

The example of a hug is beautiful and relatable. There is magic in the feel of such an embrace. But far deeper, and more meaningful, is what is unseen within this intimate exchange— the love that inspires it. That surrounds it. That is...it.

Instituted by Christ

The second component of a sacrament is that it is something that has been given to us, instituted by Christ himself. Sacraments were not invented by man; they have biblical roots in Scripture. Our Lord created (and in the case of marriage, uplifted) and gave us each of the seven sacraments during his earthly ministry.

One of the clearest examples we have of this is in the institution of the Eucharist. At the Last Supper, in his command,

"Do this in remembrance of me," Jesus clearly presents the sacrament with the desire for the disciples to continue forward with this life-giving gift.

Because Jesus not only preached often about the need for baptism but was baptized himself, there is some debate among scholars about the exact moment Jesus instituted the sacrament of baptism. According to the *Catholic Encyclopedia*, the most probable place for the institution of this sacrament was at the end of the Gospel of Matthew when Jesus commanded his apostles:

> "Go, therefore, and make disciples of all nations, baptizing them in the name of the Father, and of the Son, and of the Holy Spirit."
>
> *Matthew 28:19*

Give Grace

The third component of what comprises a sacrament is the life-giving gift it presents us with—grace. If you asked people if they wanted Gods grace, most would respond favorably. Certainly we would not be surprised to see most of the faithful in emphatic favor of it. The faithful know that grace is good. Most of us recognize and agree that grace is beneficial and is something God wants to give to us. Catholics understand that grace especially abides in and is poured from the sacraments.

But if a large group was asked to define grace, the question may incite a deer-in-the-headlights look from many.

Grace seems to be easier to internalize than it is to explain. While I believe this is the case, I can only speak for myself. Soon after my ordination, while working on a presentation, I realized how ill-prepared I might be if someone were to press me to explain grace. I might have been able to soft-pedal a few words about it: it's a gift from God; it's good; it'll make us better people, better Christians. But is this a good description of grace? No.

Knowing I had no robust response on the definition of grace, I began to research it. After a little digging, I unearthed what I considered to be a gem of descriptors. Not only did I understand it, but I could easily share it with others.

> Grace is favor, the free and undeserved help that God gives us to respond to his call to become children of God, adoptive sons, partakers of the divine nature and of eternal life.
>
> *Catechism of the Catholic Church,* 1996

Let's discuss this definition's three truths about grace:
- Grace is free and undeserved.
- Grace has a call-and-response component.
- Grace calls us to take part in the Divine and eternal life.

Free and Undeserved

"Grace is favor, the free and undeserved help that God gives us" tells us that while we do not deserve it, God freely gives us his gift of grace out of his great love for us. Grace cannot be earned. We are not owed grace because of anything we do, have done, or ever will do. Grace is a gift we can accept.

Call and Response

The second feature gave me the greatest clarity in understanding grace. It tells us what this free gift gives us: "help that God gives us to respond to his call." Two components comprise this action of grace: a call and a response.

The call, God's shout to us, is: "Listen to me! Hear from me the way to life. I love you, come this way!" God knows what is best for us, and he continually reaches out with this call to move toward him and on to a happy and abundant life.

I envision that call being like a giant radio signal being broadcast to all expanses of the planet. But forces in the world increasingly mute the signal. Evil seeks to jam the signal that broadcasts God's call. Evil intercepts the signal and renders it inaudible to its intended recipients.

As a result, God's call gets harder to hear. It gets drowned by diversions that nibble away at our happiness and seek to rob us of God's ultimate gifts. Sometimes those outside worldly influences begin to nest within us, so much so that at times we may turn down the volume ourselves or, worse, adjust the knobs to tune into other, distracting, and lifeless stations.

But with grace there is hope for restoring God's signal to its rightful place. Grace provides us with "the help (needed) to respond to his call." This is the essence of grace. The more grace we receive, the more we are empowered to hear and to respond to the constant call of life coming from God himself.

One of the best examples of this action occurs at Mass. When I am fully attentive and engaged at Mass, I feel drawn closer to God. As a result, I develop an increasingly strong desire to remain on his path of life, committed to following him in all I do. And I can foresee that if I pull back from regular Mass attendance, my response to that call would weaken over time. While God delivers his grace in many ways and through multiple channels, grace nears its zenith during the Mass, most especially within the sacrament of the Eucharist, when Christ himself becomes fully present.

Ask daily Mass-goers to describe how their daily attendance, and more specifically their receipt of daily Communion, affects their ability to not only hear God's call but to respond to it. I suspect the positive responses would overwhelm you.

Understand this about grace. It is a two-way street. To receive its maximum benefit, we must participate in it actively. James the Apostle may have put it best when he wrote one of my favorite lines of Scripture: "Draw near to God, and he will draw near to you" (James 4:8). Active participation requires possession of a clear and proper understanding of the main vehicles through which grace is delivered, the sacraments.

If you are having a difficult time relating to the intense connection I'm attempting to make between the Eucharist and the feelings of being drawn into something beyond the senses, your current understanding of the Eucharist may be the cause. Please read your way through all four relay legs. You may face little else more vital in your life than to investigate, ponder, and hopefully come to understand the true reality of the Eucharist as taught by Christ himself.

Partakers of the Divine Nature

What do we get for hearing and responding to God's call? This final part of grace clearly relates the benefit: "to become adoptive sons, partakers of the divine nature and of eternal life." Additionally, there is value beyond measure in the call itself! Grace is amazing.

Sacraments, Grace, the Eucharist

In wrapping up the topics of sacraments, grace, and the Eucharist, I hope you see how intertwined the three are. Jesus gave us the sacraments to help us receive his undeserved gift of grace. While we receive grace in many places, including through prayer, it most substantially comes to us in the sacraments. In receiving them, we are especially empowered by Christ to hear his call to become partakers in his divine life. We also receive extensive power to respond to that call. And of all the sacraments, the Eucharist—the source and summit of our Catholic faith—is the richest in outpouring of grace.

I would like to share a personal practice of mine. I was so amazed by this understanding of grace and the intensely deep relationship between grace and the Eucharist, that after receiving holy Communion, my immediate prayer became, "Lord Jesus, may the many graces contained that I received from this life-giving meal increase within me my ability to not only hear your call of love, but to ever respond to it so much more. Keep me unwavering on your path and lead me to your divine presence. I love you, Jesus. Amen."

UNDERSTANDING ESSENTIAL EUCHARISTIC DESCRIPTIONS

Like the many titles and characterizations of the Blessed Virgin Mary, numerous descriptors, definitions, and terms have been used for the Eucharist. Common ones follow.

The Real Presence of Christ

As the Pew Research data illustrates, Catholics unfortunately have greatly differing understandings of what the Eucharist is. While some view it as a symbol, representation, or memorial of the Last Supper or Christ's passion, others proclaim it to be the Real Presence of Christ himself.

Despite this division about what the Eucharist is, there is, and can only be, one authorized Church teaching on the matter. The *Catechism of the Catholic Church (CCC)*, which contains a compilation of the official teachings of the Church, says this about the Eucharist: "In the most blessed sacrament of the Eucharist, 'the body and blood, together with the soul and divinity of our Lord Jesus Christ, therefore, the whole Christ is truly, really, and substantially contained. This presence is called 'real'" (*CCC* 1374, which quotes from a document from the Council of Trent). Thus, the Church, based on the teachings of Christ, professes that the Eucharist is truly Christ fully present. It is the Real Presence of Christ himself.

For some, this presents two questions. One, how can a piece of bread and a cup of wine be divinity itself? Two, if Christ is fully present in the Eucharist, does that mean he is not present in other parts of our lives?

Jesus answers the first query, saying, "For human beings this is impossible, but for God all things are possible" (Matthew 19:26). While his comment is not specifically directed at the topic of the Eucharist, one can easily see that it applies.

A more Eucharist-centric statement is by St. Ambrose: "[If] the Word of Christ could make out of nothing that which was not; cannot it then change the things which are into that which they were not" (*De Sacramentis*, IV, 5–16)? My response is less eloquent: If God can make everything from nothing, then certainly he is capable of making himself fully present—Body, Blood, soul, and divinity—within the sacrament of holy Communion. Cannot the one who created reality, physics, and time enter into them whenever and however he chooses?

To answer the second question: While presenting to a catechetical group that Christ was fully and substantially present in the Eucharist, I was asked if that meant our Lord was then not fully present in the world outside of Mass. It's a fair question. I have often stated that God is always present to us. When we pray to him, he is with us. When we walk through the dark valleys of our lives, Christ walks beside us. The answer comes best from the words of Jesus himself. Before his ascension into heaven, he said, "And behold, I am with you always, until the end of the age" (Matthew 28:20).

I can see the potential for confusion. When we say that God is fully present in the Eucharist, "fully" can seem to imply he is less than completely present at other times. For me, this is a prime example of our finite minds trying to comprehend, and then put into words, something that is infinite, something that is beyond both words and understanding. But like the poets, still we try. The USCCB's document on the "Real Presence of Jesus Christ in the Sacrament of the Eucharist" speaks clearly on the ultra-Presence of Christ in the Eucharist:

> "This presence [of Christ in the Eucharist] is called 'real' not to exclude other types of his presence as if they could not be understood as real" (see *CCC* 1374, quoting St. Paul VI's encyclical on the Eucharist [*Mysterium Fidei*, 39]). In the sacrament of the Eucharist "the body and blood, together with the soul and divinity, of our Lord Jesus Christ and, therefore, the whole Christ is truly, really, and substantially contained."

Again, words can't always adequately describe or explain what is beyond our earthly reality. While some of the mystery described will undoubtedly get lost in any attempted translation, I hope you grasp that God's complete self is contained within God's gift of the Eucharist, his endless love and mercy. This is one of the highest opportunities for us to receive grace.

THE SOURCE AND SUMMIT OF OUR FAITH

"The mode of Christ's presence under the eucharistic species is unique, [raising] the Eucharist above all the sacraments" (*CCC* 1374). It is the most revered and perhaps the most potent conveyor of grace—above all sacraments. It stands out among the sacraments as God's favored vehicle of his love and as the most important spiritual aspect of the Catholic Church.

Of all words ever written on our faith, of all the rosaries said and prayers offered, nothing is more central to Catholicism than the Eucharist. As I have noted, the Church designates it as the "source and summit" of our faith. Ultimately, it is intended to be the source and the summit of our lives.

> The other sacraments, and indeed all ecclesiastical ministries and works of the apostolate, are bound up with the Eucharist and oriented toward it. For in the blessed Eucharist is contained the whole spiritual good of the Church, namely Christ himself, our Pasch. *CCC* 1324

Because Christ is the Eucharist and the Eucharist is Christ, nothing can be more essential or superior. Contained within the Eucharist is not only the Body, Blood, soul, and divinity of Christ, but also everything he has done for us, including his passion, death, and resurrection. To further clarify, the general consensus of the USCCB is that through his death and resurrection, Christ conquered sin and death and reconciled us to God. The Eucharist is the memorial of this sacrifice. The Church gathers to remember and to represent the sacrifice of Christ in which we share through the action of the priest and the power of the Holy Spirit. Through the celebration of the Eucharist, we are joined to Christ's sacrifice and receive its inexhaustible benefits.

The Eucharist is both a meal and a sacrifice. When we receive holy Communion, we enter into and are joined to Christ on Calvary. Through it we receive inexhaustible benefits, his grace in its most substantial form. This is why the Eucharist is so important. This is why it is essential to our continued conversion and our need to hear his call and to respond it. To say, "Yes Lord, I hear you. Draw me ever closer to you. Conform me to and in your holy will!"

TRANSUBSTANTIATION

In describing the phenomena of God deciding to break all the rules of earthly physics to gift himself to us in the humble form of bread and wine, it seems appropriate that man would come up with a scientific-sounding term to describe it. That word, eighteen letters long, is transubstantiation.

In Latin, *trans* means across. When we add *substance* to it, we come up with "across substances." Transubstantiation is the idea that describes the conversion of the bread and wine, through consecration, into the Body and Blood of Christ, with only the appearance of bread and wine remaining. Through that act of consecration by a Catholic priest, something changes among these substances. No longer are they bread and wine. They become Jesus Christ himself, Body, Blood, soul, and divinity. With God, all things are possible!

A good description of this unparalleled event comes from the Council of Trent (1545–63):

> Because Christ our Redeemer said that it was truly his body that he was offering under the species of bread, it has always been the conviction of the Church of God, and this holy Council now declares again, that by the consecration of the bread and wine there takes place a change of the whole substance of the bread into the substance of the body of Christ our Lord and of the whole substance of the wine into the substance

of his blood. The holy Catholic Church has properly called this change transubstantiation.

CCC 1376

The Council of Trent was held in response to many of the treatises of Martin Luther (1483–1546) against the Church and, of course, the fallout that followed. While his explanation of how Christ was present in the Eucharist was condemned as heretical, it is noteworthy that Martin Luther himself never wavered in his belief in Christ's Real Presence in the Eucharist. In comments on the Gospel of John 6, Luther wrote,

> All right! There we have it! This is clear, plain, and unconcealed: "I am speaking of My flesh and blood"... There we have the flat statement which cannot be interpreted in any other way than that there is no life, but death alone, apart from His flesh and blood if these are neglected or despised. How is it possible to distort this text?....You must note these words and this text with utmost diligence....It can neither speciously be interpreted nor avoided and evaded.
>
> *The Theology of Martin Luther*

Luther further clarified his belief by stating:

> Since we are confronted by God's words, "This is my body"—distinct, clear, common, definite words,

which certainly are no trope, either in Scripture or in any language—we must embrace them with faith... not as hairsplitting sophistry dictates but as God says them for us, we must repeat these words after him and hold to them.

The Theology of Martin Luther

One of Luther's contemporaries, Ulrich Zwingli, was the first to pronounce a belief in a lack of Christ's Real Presence in the Eucharist. Unlike Luther and all the teachings that preceded him back to Christ himself, Zwingli was the first to strip Jesus' words, "This is my body," of their meaning and state that our Lord was speaking symbolically. While Luther bitterly argued against Zwingli and this assertion, it has come to represent the larger Protestant narrative on the Eucharist. Let's look at this Protestant view of the Eucharist.

HOLY COMMUNION: THE PROTESTANT PERSPECTIVE

While not every Catholic believes in the Real Presence of the Eucharist, the greatest opposition to this teaching resides with our Protestant brothers and sisters, most especially within its nondenominational, or evangelical, sector. The crux of the difference is one of reality versus symbol. As to what the Eucharist is said to symbolize, most of the Protestant faithful tie it to its origin, the Last Supper. There, at the table, with the bread and wine of that Passover meal before him, Jesus took the bread, said the blessing, broke the bread, and gave it to them, saying, "'This is my body, which will be given for you; do this in memory of me.' And likewise the cup after they had eaten, saying, 'This cup is the new covenant in my blood, which will be shed for you'" (Luke 22:19–20).

These words present two concepts key to the Protestant understanding of the Eucharist. The words and concepts are "covenant" and "remembrance," both said by Jesus. At the time of Christ, "covenant" was the most important to a Jew.

A covenant is a relationship between God and man; some might call it a pact. But there is much more to it than just some type of deal or contractual agreement. It is significantly deeper, and richly familiar. Jews in the days of the Old Testament and Jesus' time understood that a covenant was a way to extend family. Thus, a covenant is God's offer to humanity to join him, to become a member of his family.

One thing to note about a covenant is that it requires absolute adherence to the covenantal relationship that is made. If either party breaks the terms, there are consequences. In his perfection, God is incapable of breaking a promise. Broken covenants have always been on humanity. God established five covenants with man during the time span of the Old Testament. Man broke every single one. Finally, God came to earth in the person of his Son, the New Covenant.

It is within this moment of salvation history that Jesus at the Last Supper, using the species of bread and wine, established with humanity the final and perfect covenant. It is at that moment that all the Christian faithful ought to cling to, to give thanks for, and to remember. This is something that Catholics and Protestants alike rejoice in!

Every covenant made by God had a sign associated with it. The Noahic covenant's sign was a rainbow. The sign of the covenant made with Adam was the sabbath. The New Covenant of Jesus is no different. The sign of Jesus' covenant is the Eucharist. Since Zwingli, the Protestant majority view has been that the Eucharist is nothing more than a sign. They view it as a point of reflection on the Last Supper and the establishment of the New Covenant.

The Protestant remembrance includes introspection and an outward communal component. While some denominations offer a Communion service as often as once a week, most evangelical churches commemorate the actions of the Last Supper, the breaking of the bread, once a month. Believing Jesus was speaking figuratively when he said, "This is my body," and, "This is my blood," most Protestant congregations move and act instead upon the words Jesus said following them, "Do this in remembrance of me." They believe the words but don't take the words that precede them literally.

In Protestant Communion services, small cubes of bread and little plastic cups of grape juice (wine is used sometimes) are passed to each member of the congregation. These tangible symbols of bread and wine then help the church members to recall the beginning of Christ's passion. Ironically, a pivotal cornerstone of the Protestant faith is the literal interpretation of Scripture—a discussion for another place and time. The key takeaway is that the Catholic position takes quite literally the words Christ spoke: "This is my body."

What I have said here is a majority view of the Protestant faithful. They especially apply when it comes to describing the beliefs of the evangelical Christian community. But with more than 35,000 Protestant denominations, I cannot accurately describe the intricacies of the differences that may exist between each sector when it comes to the Eucharist. But we must acknowledge that in larger denominations, namely Anglican and Lutheran, there is a belief that our Lord is present in the Eucharist, but not that the bread and wine have transubstantially become Christ himself.

Suffice it to say that, for Catholics, the Eucharist is the total substance of the covenant-maker himself, Jesus Christ. But don't take my word alone. What did Jesus have to say and what did he teach about his Real Presence within this covenantal sign both prior to and during the Last Supper? What did his apostles and those men who followed immediately after the apostles believe and teach? And how about the men who followed after them, including Martin Luther? I recognize that what I have to say on this topic may hold little merit. But what Jesus said, followed by what his disciples said and wrote, successfully handed off in an unbroken chain of truth one by one to the next. That should have significant value.

If you are a member a Christian denomination other than Catholic or are among the many Catholics who currently do not believe in the Real Presence, I have a twofold hope for you. First, that your curiosity has been piqued enough to continue reading. And second, that you are willing to be open to the possibility that everything described about the Eucharist thus far is true.

If you are a Catholic who believes in the Real Presence, who is open to having your faith strengthened, or who finds it difficult to explain this life-giving grace delivering mystery to others, then please also read on.

My use of the relay-race imagery is being used to accomplish both of these goals. What you will discover is that the baton has never dropped. The message of the Real Presence of the Eucharist begins with Jesus himself and has been passed on, unbroken and unchanged, through recorded history, from Christ to today.

While the teaching of the Eucharist began with and was then transmitted by Jesus, early prefigurements of its coming can be found calling out from the Old Testament. May you find these precursors as enlightening and prophetic as I do. Let's turn our attention to four such signposts from the Old Testament before moving on to Jesus' teachings.

CHAPTER 3

Eucharistic Prefigurements

I n a video synopsis of his book *Jesus and the Jewish Roots of the Eucharist: Unlocking the Secrets of the Last Supper,* author Brant Pitre, a distinguished research professor of Scripture at the Augustine Institute, explains that the more intimately we relate with the Jewish tradition as we seek to understand the Christian faith, the more likely we will be to understand why the Catholic Church teaches that the Eucharist is the "source and summit of the Christian life."

Without question, one of the most effective ways to understand the teachings of Jesus and his apostles is to review the writings of the New Testament with the perspective of a first-century Jew. So much of what is being communicated can become lost if we do not have an accurate understanding of the time, history, and culture of what we are reading. The parables of Jesus are a good example. Without scholarly guidance on things like the nature of storytelling, the political landscape, the context of customs and traditions, etc., of the times we are reading about, we will likely come away with inaccurate interpretations. While parables prove particularly tricky to understand, these same principles apply on how to best read and interpret all stories of the Bible.

For this reason, we look back to the perspectives and experiences of the immediate, contemporary audiences of Jesus. In doing so, we may come to understand why the first Christians readily took to the belief that the Eucharist was truly Christ himself. They recognized that the Eucharist was the fulfillment of many of the writings of the Old Testament.

Eucharistic prefigurements are those events or people that pointed to the Eucharist well before the time of Jesus. Our focus will center on four Old Testament staples:

- Melchizedek
- The Passover
- Manna
- Showbread/Bread of Presence

If you have ever wondered why Jesus chose something as simple as bread and wine to become the gift of his total being, this next section should be enlightening.

MELCHIZEDEK

If you have been to Mass, you have likely heard Melchizedek mentioned. His name is said shortly after the consecration during Eucharistic Prayer 1: "Be pleased to look upon these offerings with a serene and kindly countenance, and to accept them, as once you were pleased to accept the gifts of your servant Abel the Just, the sacrifice of Abraham, our father in faith, and the offering of your high priest Melchizedek, a holy sacrifice, a spotless victim."

While the stories of Abraham and Abel are likely familiar, those of Melchizedek often tend to fly under most Christian radars. There is good reason for this—he is only mentioned, briefly, three times in the Bible: in Genesis, Psalm 110, and the Letter to the Hebrews. Melchizedek appears early in the

Old Testament when he mysteriously intersects with Abram (not yet renamed by God as Abraham), as he is returning from a key battlefield victory.

The Book of Genesis states that "Melchizedek, king of Salem, brought out bread and wine. He was a priest of God Most High. He blessed Abram with these words, 'Blessed be Abram by God the Most High, the creator of heaven and earth; And blessed be God the Most High, who delivered your foes into your hand.'" Then Abram gave him a tenth of everything (Genesis 14:18–20).

This introduction to Melchizedek raises questions. Who was Melchizedek? How did he know Abram? Did Abram know him, or was this their first encounter? But none of them help our cause in seeking a connection between Melchizedek, Jesus, and the Eucharist. However, several things within this brief narrative provide significant insight into Melchizedek's importance and his relationship to Jesus and the Eucharist.

The first is found in the blessing in Genesis 14:19–20. Melchizedek blesses Abram, apparently following the custom of the time that the greater always blesses the lesser. Also notice how the encounter between these two men ends with Abram tithing Melchizedek. Like the blessing, Abram giving ten percent of all he owns to Melchizedek is a gesture of subservience. In light of the important role Abraham plays in salvation history, these two occurrences give vital insights into the stature and importance of Melchizedek.

In the Genesis narrative of Melchizedek, the two things

that perhaps most connect this man with Jesus and the Eucharist are his gift of bread and wine and the mention thereafter of his priesthood to God the Most High. Also interesting is that the Jewish priesthood as we know it did not begin for another thousand years, with the ordination of Aaron. Since his is not a Jewish priesthood, it tells us Melchizedek's priesthood is one for all humanity. In Psalm 110 we learn it is also a priesthood for all time: "You are a Priest forever in the manner of Melchizedek" (Psalm 110:4).

This verse from Psalm 110 is also heavily reflected on in the Book of Hebrews. The author positions this verse as a prophetic prefigurement of Christ. Jesus, who also is indeed a priest for all humanity, not just the Jews, and a priest for all time (Hebrews 7:22–28). And lest we forget, what did Jesus offer as a sacrifice at the Last Supper? Bread and wine.

Also, "in the manner of Melchizedek" in Psalm 110 does not just mean Jesus emulated the action of Melchizedek. Rather, it suggests Christ was instituting a priesthood like Melchizedek's, one that did not require an offering of animal blood sacrifice but a sacrifice of bread and wine.

Returning to the introduction of Melchizedek in Genesis, we find a final observation from the text worth mentioning. The first description of him says he is a priest and a king from Salem. Psalm 76:3 says Salem refers to Zion, which is synonymous with Jerusalem. Thus, Melchizedek is a priest and king of the city where Jesus institutes the Eucharist, the city where Jesus is crucified under the title "King of the Jews." From

Melchizedek's own city of origin came Jesus, a king and a priest of the Most High God, a priest for all humanity whose sacrificial offering was also bread and wine.

Concluding this section on Melchizedek's relationship to Christ and the Eucharist is a summary from the *Catechism* (1544):

> Everything that the priesthood of the Old Covenant prefigured finds its fulfillment in Christ Jesus, the "one mediator between God and men." The Christian tradition considers Melchizedek, "priest of God Most High," as a prefiguration of the priesthood of Christ, the unique "high priest after the order of Melchizedek"; "holy, blameless, unstained"; "by a single offering he has perfected for all time those who are sanctified," that is, by the unique sacrifice of the cross.

It seems significant that Jesus chooses to offer the gifts of bread and wine in his priesthood at the first sacrifice of the Mass and from then on. As we will see, Melchizedek's early prefigurement to the Eucharist doesn't stand alone.

THE PASSOVER

The Last Supper was the site of both the institution of the Eucharist and the birthplace of the New Covenant. But to Jesus' guests that evening, it started as only one thing—a celebration of the Passover. That evening, Jesus did not precisely follow the traditional Passover script. Not only did he add content to the Passover meal, but he also seemingly forgot to present and consume the meal's fourth cup: the Cup of Praise. Based on these irregularities, I imagine his apostles likely would have stayed highly focused on all the actions and words of Jesus that night. But nonetheless, this was still a Passover meal. As such, it is impossible to separate the Last Supper, or more precisely to us, the institution of the Eucharist, from the origins of the Old Testament Passover.

The Passover is a remembrance of the events that led to the Exodus, the Jewish people's freedom from slavery in Egypt. The tipping point came after Pharaoh, despite suffering nine horrendous plagues for his noncompliance to Moses' commands (made on behalf of God), still refused to free the Jews from bondage. Moses gave Pharaoh a final chance to free his slaves; if he refused, he was told that all firstborn sons in Egypt, including those from Jewish families would be killed. There was one caveat. Moses instructed the Jews to sprinkle the blood from a lamb, sacrificed for this purpose, on the doorway of their homes. With this marking, their homes and all the firstborn within would be "passed over" from the life-ending effects of the tenth plague.

From then to today, Jews commemorate this event through the celebration of the Passover. Today, this involves only a meal. Up until the destruction of the Temple in the year 70, the Jewish Passover had two components: a sacrifice at the temple where a lamb would be offered, followed by a meal, which included the eating of the sacrificed lamb by a family.

Both the sacrifice and meal had a designated leader. At the temple, only one person could offer sacrifices, a priest. At home, the Passover meal, along with its scripted components, are led by the father of the family. Based on these initial introductions to the Passover, a couple of significant connections to Jesus appear. Jesus is the designated leader of not only the meal but, in his priestly role, also the sacrifice to come. In addition, Jesus himself is the sacrifice. He is the lamb who is prefigured in the story of the Exodus.

During the Passover meal, the eldest son asks his father four questions about the Exodus, including: "Why is it that on all other nights we eat leavened bread?" The answer? Because they had to leave Egypt so quickly, they did not have time to let the dough rise. More significant to us is what Jesus did with the unleavened bread on the night of the Last Supper. Rather than providing the usual explanation for its flatness, he held it up and diverted from the Passover script, saying, "This is my body." He was not recalling or reflecting on anything from the past, and he certainly was not saying anything like, "This bread is like my body." He explicitly says, "This *is* my body."

Four cups of wine are presented during the Passover meal. Like the unleavened bread, each cup plays an important role in telling the story of the Exodus and the hope for the coming of the Messiah. During the meal, each cup is presented at a designated time and stories are told. At the Last Supper, Jesus took a cup (believed to be the third) of the Passover meal called "the Cup of Redemption." The redemption component of this cup is based on Exodus 6:6, "I will redeem you by my outstretched arm and with mighty acts of judgment."

Because the Jews of Moses' time were rescued and redeemed from their slavery in Egypt, since that time this third Passover cup has been offered in prayer for the ultimate redemption that would come from the Messiah. It was with this Cup of Redemption that Jesus instituted the new and everlasting covenant. The anticipated Messiah, now present, makes known the redemptive purpose of this sacred and beloved third cup of the Passover with the words: "for this is my blood of the covenant, which will be shed on behalf of many for the forgiveness of sins" (Matthew 26:28).

Note how the Passover foreshadowed and pointed to the Eucharist, to the bread and wine of the Last Supper. As we look more into the past, we see that Jesus' choice of bread and wine as the substances to which he makes himself manifest for all time was intentional. It connects perfectly in a divine symphony to that which appears to have eternal origins. His bread is indeed the Bread of Life, and his cup is indeed the Cup of Redemption. Speaking of heavenly, let's take a look into the original bread of heaven, God's gift of manna.

MANNA

"What is this?" is the meaning of the Hebrew word *manna*. Since none of the Jews who left Egypt knew what this life-sustaining, breadlike substance was, they could account for it in only one way: it was a miracle, a gift of life from God to them.

The occurrence of manna begins soon after the Jews narrowly escaped Pharaoh's attempt to kill them in the Red Sea. Shortly after witnessing this miracle at the Red Sea, the people of Israel began to complain in the desert against Moses and Aaron. The Israelites said to them in Exodus 16:3:

> If only we had died at the LORD's hand in the land of Egypt, as we sat by our kettles of meat and ate our fill of bread! But you have led us into this wilderness to make this whole assembly die of famine!

This account may be hard to fathom. How could these people be so unappreciative, complaining so quickly after having their lives just saved by God in such a dramatic way? Surely having the water part so one can walk through an entire sea before collapsing on the enemy the moment they were out of harm's way deserved some gratitude! Thankfully, God is the epitome of patience. In his great love and inexplicable tolerance, he responded to the Israelites with yet another miracle:

Then the LORD said to Moses, "I am going to rain down bread from heaven for you. Each day the people are to go out and gather their daily portion...." On seeing it, the Israelites asked one another, "What is this?" for they did not know what it was. But Moses told them, "It is the bread which the LORD has given you to eat."

Exodus 16:4a, 15

Out of nowhere, the hand of God provides (in abundance) manna, bread from heaven for his people. Each person was told to collect about nine cups of manna (an *omer*) to eat throughout the day. This food was delivered to them every morning for the next forty years, until they finally made it into the Promised Land.

Moses said, "This is what the LORD has commanded. Keep a full omer of it for future generations, so that they may see what food I gave you to eat in the wilderness when I brought you out of the land of Egypt." Moses then told Aaron, "Take a jar and put a full omer of manna in it. Then place it before the Lord to keep it for future generations." As the LORD had commanded Moses, Aaron placed it in front of the covenant to keep it.

Exodus 16:32–34

This is revealing. God is specifically asking to have some of the manna put aside so that future generations of Israel can see for themselves the miracle he had provided his people. Where it was placed is significant: next to the Ten Commandments in the Ark of the Covenant, which is then stored in the Holy of Holies. Thus, this manna is not only physical fuel needed by the people for their journey, but it is holy food as well! The most revered space of the Ark of the Covenant was reserved for the holiest items in all of Jewish history: the Ten Commandments, Aaron's staff that Moses used to perform miracles, and now an omer of manna.

If the placement of this bread sounds familiar, it should. Where is the miracle bread of our faith housed? In the tabernacle, our modern-day ark. And the tabernacle is found in the sanctuary in churches, our modern-day Holy of Holies. If these relationships between manna and the Eucharist are not yet enough to have you concede a strong heavenly connection between the two, then consider how Brant Pitre's previously mentioned book on the Jewish roots of the Eucharist reinforces the connection between rabbinic and Old Testament writings and the Eucharist. In chapter four, aptly titled "The Manna of the Messiah," Pitre points to ancient Jewish teachings, coming from outside the Old Testament, that the future Messiah would bring back with him the miracle of manna. Some of those writings follow.

According to *Midrash Rabbah* by Rabbi David Adani of Yemen in the fourteenth century, just as the first redeemer caused manna to descend, "I am going to rain down bread from heaven for you" (Exodus 16:4), so too will the later redeemer cause manna to descend. Pitre says this means that just as Moses, through the work of God, gave the nomadic Israelites manna from heaven, so also would the Messiah, the new Moses, when he comes. Since the Redeemer, the Messiah, is Jesus, it isn't much of a leap to see his Eucharist as the new manna.

Pitre's second supporting reference comes from the second-century Rabbi Ishmael, who says the manna will not be found in his own age but in the age to come. Pitre points out that, in Jewish thinking, "the age to come" referred to the messianic age, to the coming of the Messiah. They believed his coming would bring with it the return of the miraculous manna.

Is this discussion of manna and bread a coincidence? Is it serendipitous that Jewish rabbis, independent and distant of any Christian tradition, linked the return of manna to the coming of the Messiah? Christians share in the belief that the Messiah did come. Catholic Christians also believe that when he came, he once again elevated the simple substance of bread to the highest heights of holiness.

SHOWBREAD/BREAD OF PRESENCE

A fascinating facet about our final prefigurements of the Eucharist is in its name. The Hebrew name given for another special bread of our Jewish ancestors is *lechem ha panim:* "Bread of the Face." Whose face is being referred to? If you guessed God's face, you are correct. It also goes by two other titles: the Bread of the Presence and Showbread (also referred to as Shewbread). Whether contained in an action or tied up in covenant language, these three names provide us both an understanding of what this bread represented, as well as what it reveals to us about its connection with the Eucharist.

In looking into these three titles, let's first examine two Old Testament writings. The first biblical reference to Showbread is found in Exodus 25. This chapter outlines the construction of the Tabernacle and the items that were to be placed in it. These next verses from Exodus 25 describe the construction of the table that this bread is to be set upon and other utensils that were to accompany it:

> You shall also make a table of acacia wood, two cubits long, a cubit wide, and a cubit and a half high. Plate it with pure gold and make a molding of gold around it. Make a frame for it, a handbreadth high, and make a molding of gold around the frame. You shall also make four rings of gold for it and fasten them at the four corners, one at each leg. The rings shall be along-

side the frame as holders for the poles to carry the table. These poles for carrying the table you shall make of acacia wood and plate with gold. You shall make its plates and cups, as well as its pitchers and bowls for pouring libations; make them of pure gold. On the table you shall always keep Showbread set before me.

Exodus 25:23–30

This passage mentions several noteworthy items. First, God gives instructions to Moses on the construction of this table. The fact that the Almighty gives the instructions and requests a precious metal, pure gold, dictates that the table and what is put on it are to be considered very holy. Also note that only three things were to go into the sanctuary, the holiest of places: the Ark of the Covenant, the Golden Lampstand (Menorah), and the table of the Bread of the Presence.

Also of interest is God's direction to create gold "pitchers and bowls for pouring libations in," to be set on the table next to the Showbread. Libations mean wine. Thus, wine is always to be joined with this special bread. Note the last line, "On the table you shall always keep Showbread set before me." This offering to the Lord is to be perpetual, a never-ending offering to God on High.

Now that we have a table on which to place this bread and the libations that accompany it, let's examine exactly what this bread is and its purpose.

Take bran flour and bake it into twelve cakes, using two-tenths of an ephah of flour for each cake. These you shall place in two piles, six in each pile, on the pure gold table before the LORD. With each pile put some pure frankincense, which shall serve as an oblation to the LORD, a token of the bread offering. Regularly on each Sabbath day, the bread shall be set out before the LORD on behalf of the Israelites by an everlasting covenant. It shall belong to Aaron and his sons, who must eat it in a sacred place, since it is most sacred, his as a perpetual due from the oblations to the LORD.

Leviticus 24:5–9

Showbread is twelve cakes or loaves of bread that serve as a bloodless sacrifice/oblation to God. Like Exodus, the Book of Leviticus points out that what is being described is more than just a sacrifice—it is a representation of an "everlasting covenant" between God and the Israelites. Fast-forward thousands of years and we have Jesus, our high priest, establishing the new and everlasting covenant with the sign of bread.

These twelve loaves of bread, symbolizing the twelve tribes of Israel, were prepared by the priests for each Sabbath. Thus they held a principal role in early Jewish worship. The bread was considered sacred and could only be consumed by the high priests and the priest who worked within the tabernacle, and/or future temple, during that week. The priests would eat the bread of the "Presence" at the golden table, within the tabernacle space, thereby consuming it in the "presence" of God.

While we may now have an explanation for the title, the Bread of the Presence, let us turn here to the meaning of Showbread and its connection to the Bread of the Face. It was customary for Jewish men to go to Jerusalem three times a year to attend the feasts of Tabernacles, Passover, and Weeks. During these special feasts, the Jewish faithful were treated to something unique and quite special. Since only priests were allowed to enter into the sanctuary of the Temple, they were the only ones who set eyes upon the sacred items contained within. On these feast days, however, the priest at the Temple would bring out the Showbread for the Jewish people to see. The priest would elevate the bread and say, "Behold God's love for you!" These words make sense. Again, the Bread of the Presence was a sign of their covenant with God. And covenants, beyond all else, are bonds of love.

In being "shown" this bread, the Jews believed they were standing before the Presence of God, many feeling as though they were seeing *lechem ha panim*, "the Face of God," or as much as they could of his earthly presence. No matter what title we attach to it—Showbread, Bread of the Face, or Bread of the Presence—it is impossible to escape the similarities between these Old Testament beliefs and practices and our modern experience with the sacrament of the Eucharist. Though the original bread was consumed by the priest on the gold table in the holiest of places of their time, today the Eucharist is presented at our altars and is for the faithful to eat. Finally, while the Bread of the Presence was a symbol of a covenant with the Almighty for the Jews, for Catholics the Eucharist is more than a mere sign: it is Christ himself in total.

PREFIGUREMENTS SUMMARY

When we examine the relationships between the Eucharist and the Old Testament to Melchizedek, the Passover, manna, and the Bread of the Presence, we see that God's plan of salvation is unquestionably rooted in the Jewish heritage of our faith. To ignore this history would be to settle for a limited understanding of the life and passion of Jesus.

Upon understanding this, we see the carefully considered sensibility of Jesus' choice of simple bread and wine to become his complete person: Body, Blood, soul, and divinity. All the pieces of the puzzle fit when we make the effort to pan our cameras out, from our singular Christian perspective to a much wider, Jewish-inclusive view of all of salvation history.

One final note before diving into the relay. Under each leg, you will find a lot of information. There is so much that you might want to say, "I thought you said this metaphor will make explaining the Real Presence of the Eucharist simple!" At the end of the book, I will show how a simple explanation is easily accomplished. For now, know that the simplicity lies in recalling and using the imagery of a relay race.

CHAPTER 4

Leg One:
The Teachings of Jesus

I liken the prefigurements of the Eucharist to two things: an overzealous sports promoter and the actual event that he or she is hyping to attract ticket buyers. Weeks before the event, signs are posted around town publicizing the event's date and location. Direct-mail pieces remind recipients to "mark your calendar." Radio stations broadcast the details. The marketing efforts—the foreshadowing of the event—is intended to send a less-than-subtle message to "take heed! What I'm promoting is worth it!"

Chapter three was all about those signs. I hope your anticipation for what they point to has grown. In metaphoric terms, the event is the eucharistic relay race based on one person, Jesus Christ. It cannot be overstated: leg one of our race, which Christ ran, is by far the most important. Without it, there would be no race. Because it centers on the source of all eucharistic teachings, this chapter/relay leg is longer and more comprehensive than the remaining three.

The teaching of Jesus begins our search for the true meaning of the Eucharist in earnest. This chapter offers a thorough examination of what the person who first presented it, instituted it, and actually exemplifies it had to say about it. This first leg focuses on three places where Jesus makes clear what the Eucharist is:

- John 6
- The Last Supper
- The Lord's Prayer

JOHN CHAPTER 6

John 6, with seventy-one verses, contains three episodes:

- The Multiplication of the Loaves
- Jesus Walking on the Water
- The Bread of Life Discourse

While the Bread of Life Discourse is certainly the central focus of the first leg of our relay analogy, the other two accounts, particularly the first, help lay the foundation for the third and final explanation of this section.

MULTIPLICATION OF THE LOAVES

What jumps out immediately from this occurrence is that, once again, something miraculous happens involving bread. All four Gospel writers record this event and note the crowd size (5,000). Commonly at the time, only men were counted, so the total size, including women and children, was likely 10,000-plus. The location, across the Sea of Galilee, was across from the ministry's base town, Capernaum.

Significant in the passage is what is said about this crowd as the chapter opens: "A large crowd followed him" (John 6:2). Understand, this crowd had not just congregated because of a preplanned event. A great many had been following Jesus, some for days, others for weeks, and many for longer periods.

Due to his words, miracles, and an overall fascination, these people—who were disciples of Jesus—made it a priority to shadow him most everywhere he went.

After looking over the crowd that day, Jesus, filled with compassion and to test his appointed apostles, asks Philip where they could get enough food to feed the enormous flock. You probably know the rest of the story. Andrew locates a boy who has two fish and five loaves of bread. Jesus blesses the offering, and his disciples distribute the food to the people. Lo and behold, after everyone has eaten their fill, there are still twelve full baskets of leftovers!

While this large gathering of followers had seen many miracles performed by Jesus in the past, this one appears to really get them energized. So much so that the Scripture story ends by telling us that the crowd was coming to carry him off to make him king. Jesus, having none of it, withdraws alone to the mountain.

It is fascinating that just the day before Jesus' crucial teaching on the Eucharist, we have a miracle related to, of all things, bread. As a primer for the upcoming discussion on the Bread of Life Discourse, remember three things from this account that we'll return to:

- The number of disciples present
- The disciples' fervent devotion to him
- The disciples' desire to make him king

WALKING ON WATER

Something interesting occurs within this short narrative: Jesus' disciples leave by boat from where Jesus had fed the multitude to travel to Capernaum without Jesus. One can assume that Jesus had directed them to do so. Three to four miles into their journey, they hit a storm. Amid the mounting waves, Jesus walks on the sea toward them. What he says next and what subsequently happens amazes them. Both amaze us today. Jesus says:

> "It is I. Do not be afraid." They wanted to take him into the boat, but the boat immediately arrived at the shore to which they were heading.
>
> *John 6:20–21*

While the boat making it immediately to shore after Jesus speaks is astounding, more revealing and of greater importance are the immediate words Jesus speaks to them: "It is I," which translates to, "I am," the unspoken name of God. Having just witnessed Jesus walking on water and going instantaneously from storm to shore, I doubt anyone in that boat had a problem believing Jesus' declaration of divinity.

In sum, on the heels of one of his most important teachings, right after performing a miracle involving bread, and right before he delivers one of his most essential teachings, he again reveals to his disciples his divine nature. Coincidence?

THE BREAD OF LIFE DISCOURSE

At forty-nine verses, the Bread of Life Discourse (John 6:22–71) comprises more than half of the entire chapter and provides a critical eucharistic link. I'll break down its content into three sections:

- Background Leading to the Key Teaching on the Eucharist
- The Immediate Results of the Teaching
- Unpacking the Teachings

BACKGROUND

The events of the Bread of Life Discourse occur in Capernaum the day following the Feeding of the 5,000. When people in great crowd awake that next day, they discover Jesus and his closest followers have left, unnoticed by anyone. Many from that large throng pile into boats and sail to Capernaum, where they find Jesus. Given the commitment of the crowd, especially having been stirred the day before to the point of wanting to make him king, we can imagine that many thousands came to Capernaum that day in search of Jesus. There they find him and engage with him:

> So they said to him, "What can we do to accomplish the works of God?" Jesus answered and said to them,

"This is the work of God, that you believe in the one he sent." So they said to him, "What sign can you do, that we may see and believe in you? What can you do? Our ancestors ate manna in the desert, as it is written: 'He gave them bread from heaven to eat.'"

John 6:28–31

It's interesting that the crowd asks for a sign so they can believe in Jesus. This comes right after seeing a miracle the day before that made them want to hoist Jesus on their shoulders and make him king. It's also intriguing that they immediately refer to their ancestors receiving manna in the desert. The pieces of this great puzzle about the Eucharist are beginning to fall together. Jesus responds to the crowd's request:

"Amen, amen, I say to you, it was not Moses who gave the bread from heaven; my Father gives you the true bread from heaven." ...So, they said to him, "Sir, give us this bread always." Jesus said to them, "I am the bread of life; whoever comes to me will never hunger, and whoever believes in me will never thirst."

John 6:32, 34–35

Notice the first thing Jesus does is correct the people's assertion that Moses provided manna for forty years in the desert. God the Father provided the bread from heaven, not Moses. The crowd seems so satisfied with his answer that they not only ask for some of this bread, but that they receive it "always." That leads into Jesus' proclamation that he is the Bread of Life and that whoever believes in him will "never hunger" and "never thirst."

Jesus follows this by claiming he is the "bread that came down from heaven" and that he holds the key to eternal life. The crowd realizes at this point that he is no longer promising free and endless bread. More than a providential handout, they now understand he is making a radical claim of divinity. Understandably, those gathered begin to feel a little uneasy as his discourse in John continues:

> "Because I came down from heaven not to do my own will but the will of the one who sent me....For this is the will of my Father, that everyone who sees the Son and believes in him may have eternal life, and I shall raise him [on] the last day." The Jews murmured about him because he said, "I am the bread that came down from heaven," and they said, "Is this not Jesus, the son of Joseph? Do we not know his father and mother? Then how can he say, 'I have come down from heaven'?" Jesus answered and said to them, "Stop murmuring among yourselves. No one can come to me unless the Father who sent me draw him, and I will raise him on the last day. It is written in the prophets: 'They shall all be taught by God.'"
>
> *John 6:38, 40–46*

Jesus—indeed, God—does what he had just referenced from the words of Isaiah and Jeremiah in the parting statement of this quotation. He, God, is the one now teaching them. The assembled, many of whom had dropped everything and followed Jesus everywhere he went, are getting increasingly uncomfortable with what he is saying. I can imagine them feeling as though they had a school of fish tails flopping in their stomachs, accompanied by the nausea and lightheadedness that follows continuous waves of confusion.

But what Jesus says is so important, so life-giving, that he continues on and takes the conversation to another level (see John 6:45–52). He goes from suggesting he can provide the disciples an endless supply of food to proclaiming that he came down from heaven to offer eternal life, to now saying the means of achieving this is to eat this bread, which is him. The crowd's anxieties and confusion accelerate. Their great teacher, healer, miracle worker, king-in-waiting, appears to be saying crazy things. Not backing down, Jesus presses on:

> "Everyone who listens to my Father and learns from him comes to me. Not that anyone has seen the Father except the one who is from God; he has seen the Father. Amen, amen, I say to you, whoever believes has eternal life.
>
> I am the bread of life. Your ancestors ate the manna in the desert, but they died. This is the bread that

comes down from heaven so that one may eat it and not die...I am the living bread that came down from heaven; whoever eats this bread will live forever; and the bread that I will give is my flesh for the life of the world." The Jews quarreled among themselves, saying, "How can this man give us [his] flesh to eat?"

John 6:45–52

What follows is no casual mention. Jesus makes certain that what is required to receive his gift of everlasting bread, of eternal life, is for his followers to eat his flesh and drink his blood. In the span of six verses (John 6:51–56), in repetitive fashion, Jesus commands this not once but four times:

John 6:51: "...And the bread that I will give is my flesh for the life of the world."

John 6:53: "...Unless you eat the flesh of the Son of Man and drink his blood, you do not have life within you."

John 6:54: "Whoever eats my flesh and drinks my blood has eternal life, and I will raise him on the last day."

John 6:56: "For whoever eats my flesh and drinks my blood remains in me and I in him."

Those hearing Jesus had a right to be confused by him. Jewish dietary laws prohibit the eating of flesh that contained blood...let alone eating blood or the flesh and blood of a man.

Still, this teaching is so important that it had to be said. Time was running out. Jerusalem was nearing. One would hope that Jesus had earned enough trust that those listening would have remained and listened. Had they not heard enough wisdom from him? Had they not witnessed enough miracles, achieved at his hands, to accept what he had to say?

THE IMMEDIATE RESULTS
OF THE TEACHING

Despite following Jesus around for extended periods, many of those who were there that day turned and walked away from him because of this single teaching.

Given the number of people recorded as being present the day before, there were potentially thousands of disciples who turned at that moment and left Jesus. We can be thankful that Jesus had earned the trust of his twelve closest friends:

Jesus then said to the Twelve, "Do you also want to leave?" Simon Peter answered him, "Master, to whom shall we go? You have the words of eternal life. We have come to believe and are convinced that you are the Holy One of God."

John 6:67–69

UNPACKING THE TEACHING

John 6 is at the epicenter of Jesus' teaching on what the Eucharist is and the grace-filled benefits that result through it. Despite this, there is perhaps no greater theological divide between Catholics and evangelical Protestants than this chapter. Catholics take Jesus literally when he speaks in John 6, while evangelicals, who take a literal interpretation of most of Scripture, choose in this instance to believe that Jesus was speaking metaphorically.

What is at stake here is significant. If the Catholic understanding of the Eucharist is true, how could anyone, Catholic or Protestant, not want to witness Jesus making himself present at every Mass? How could anyone not want to follow Jesus' direction to take within oneself the substance of Christ and to receive the abundance of grace, "the help God gives us to respond to his call" that comes from it (*CCC* 1996)?

If the Catholic belief about the Eucharist is true, then accepting it is the only response that makes sense. For Catholics who attend Mass and do not believe in the Real Presence, this revealed truth should make them hunger for their next Mass like never before. If Jesus meant what he said, particularly in John 6:51–56, Protestants should consider coming to the only faith that provides the means for this miracle.

All of this potential, this supposition, rests on the question: Was Jesus speaking literally or symbolically? We now take on this question.

A LITERAL INTERPRETATION
(JOHN 6)

Perhaps the most convincing argument for a literal translation for the Bread of Life Discourse can be heard within the sweet and beautifully colored feathers of a bird found in rain forests throughout the world, the trogon. These gorgeous birds received their name because of their habit of gnawing holes in trees to make their nest. In Greek, *trogon* means gnawing or nibbling. We will examine the use of Greek words in the rest of this chapter. While Jesus and his followers spoke Aramaic, the earliest available New Testament writings are in Greek.

In any language, there are multiple ways to express or describe an object or action. Look at the choices we have to describe the immediate male person we are descended from. We can call this person father, dad, pops, daddy, my biological father, etc. Each conveys something a little different. For instance, the word Jesus used to describe God the Father is *Abba*, which best translates as "Daddy." This word choice connotes an intimate bond, something significantly more meaningful than a mere genetic relationship. Jesus' preference for "Abba" gives us deep insight and understanding into not only Jesus' own relationship with the Father, but also the connection he desires for us to have with the Father.

Like *Abba, trogon* reveals much about whether Jesus is speaking literally or symbolically. John 6 uses the word for *eat* fifteen times. However, two different Greek words are used for *eat* over those many citations. One is *phago*, the other is *trogon*. As mentioned, like the action of the bird, *trogon* translates best as "gnaw, crunch, or chew."

Phago, on the other hand, translates best as the less-specific, general term: "to eat." As with countless other words or phrases, depending on the context it is used in, "to eat" can be taken to mean different things. "I'm so hungry I could eat a horse" differs from "get a bite to eat." To understand what Jesus meant, one must look at both the choice of words used by the early Greek translators to best match Jesus' Aramaic and the context in which his words are used.

Of the fifteen references in John 6 to eating, *phago* is used eleven times and *trogon,* four. The key to understanding that Jesus was speaking literally versus metaphorically lies in when and in what context these two words are used.

John 6:5 When Jesus raised his eyes and saw that a large crowd was coming to him, he said to Philip, "Where can we buy enough food for them to eat?" (phago)

John 6:23 ...Boats came from Tiberias near the place where they had eaten (phago) the bread when the Lord gave thanks.

John 6:26 Jesus...said, "Amen, amen, I say to you, you are looking for me not because you saw signs but because you ate (phago) the loaves and were filled."

John 6:31 [The Jews said,] "Our ancestors ate (phago) manna in the desert, as it is written."

John 6:49 [Jesus said,] "Your ancestors ate (phago) the manna in the desert, but they died."

John 6:50 "This is the bread that comes down from heaven so that one may eat (phago) it and not die."

John 6:51 "I am the living bread that came down from heaven; whoever eats (phago) this bread will live forever; and the bread that I will give is my flesh for the life of the world."

John 6:52 The Jews quarreled among themselves, saying, "How can this man give us [his] flesh to eat (phago)?"

John 6:53 Jesus said..., "Amen, amen, I say to you, unless you eat (phago) the flesh of the Son of Man and drink his blood, you do not have life within you."

John 6:54 "Whoever eats (trogon) my flesh and drinks my blood has eternal life, and I will raise him on the last day."

John 6:56 "Whoever eats (trogon) my flesh and drinks my blood remains in me and I in him."

John 6:57 "Just as the living Father sent me and I have life because of the father, so also the one who feeds (trogon) on me will have life because of me."

John 6:58 "This is the bread that came down from heaven. Unlike your ancestors who ate (phago) and still died, whoever eats (trogon) this bread will live forever."

When Jesus refers to eating in general, anything that is unrelated to himself, the word *phago* is used. But when eating involves Jesus directly: "who eats my flesh," "the one who feeds on me," the word for "gnaw" is used. Why wouldn't Jesus stick with phago?

Jesus wants to ensure that the audience then and now understands he is speaking literally. One must eat his flesh in order to receive the graces he alone has to offer. And it is not only his simple use of the word for gnaw that is revealing, but notice as well how Jesus "quadruples down" his assertion and use of the word *gnaw*. Reread verses 54, 56, 57, and 58, only this time when you get the word *eat* in each verse, replace *eat* with the word *gnaw*.

Now place yourself in the narrative as part of the audience in Capernaum. What would you think if you heard Jesus use the word *eat* so often during a short teaching and then suddenly shift to the word *gnaw* when it comes to his person? Logically, he is being literal. And there is more. The word *trogon* appears only six times in the Bible, all in the New Testament (four in John 6). Far from overused, Jesus' use of *trogon* cannot be underscored enough.

"To eat" can mean different things, including symbolic things. "Eating someone's dust" means outperforming or outrunning someone. But when Jesus says "trogon" (to gnaw), he is being literal, not symbolic. In fact, *trogon* is never used figuratively or symbolically in any writings up to the time of Christ. That word always relates to the nature of eating—the gnawing or chewing of food. The word in pre-Christian literature is found in Homer's *Odyssey*, Aristophanes' *The Acharnians*, and *On the False Embassy* by Demosthenes. In all cases, *trogon* means to gnaw or chew food.

SARX VERSUS SOMA

A skeptic might argue: "Maybe Jesus did mean to eat or gnaw his flesh literally, but perhaps he was talking about his flesh in a symbolic way, that he was not talking about his literal flesh."

This counterargument holds no weight. The word Jesus uses in the Gospel of John for "flesh" is translated to the Greek word *sarx*. As cited and defined in both the (heavily Protestant) *Strong's* and *Thayer's Concordances*, there is little to no doubt that flesh in this context is the actual flesh of a living being: "Flesh (as stripped of the skin) that is (strictly) the meat of an animal (as food) or (by extension) the body (as opposed to the soul or spirit)" (*Strong's Concordance*).

"Flesh (the soft substance of the living body, which covers the bones and is permeated with blood) of both man and beasts" (*Thayer's Concordance*). Had Jesus desired to be abstract or symbolic, he could have used the Greek word for the body, *soma*, which is often used in symbolic terms.

Based on Catholic and Protestant interpretations of the use of the word *sarx*, we must conclude that Jesus is speaking literally about his flesh being the food of the Eucharist.

While on the topic of flesh, perhaps the most frequently used Protestant argument that Jesus is speaking metaphorically of his own flesh/sarx follows: "It is the spirit that gives life, while the flesh is of no avail. The words I have spoken to you are of spirit and life" (John 6:63).

As noted in the next section, if this was Jesus' attempt to clear up for his audience any misunderstanding that he had indeed been talking earlier about his own actual flesh, then he did a terrible job, as many disciples abandoned him immediately following this so-called explanation.

For a more crucial clarifier to the assertion that Jesus is talking about "the flesh" and not "his flesh," consider the different use of "the flesh" between John 6:63 and its use in verses 51, 53, 54, and 56. In these verses, he speaks specifically about his own flesh. If he said in John 6:63 that "his flesh" was of no avail, then everything he had just said in the Bread of Life Discourse—that eating his flesh was essential for life— would have been canceled out. Of even greater importance is that if he said, or meant, that "his flesh" was of no avail, that it was worthless, then his complete role in salvation history would have been canceled out! Without the cross, without his flesh upon it, all of Christianity would be rendered null.

A key aspect of "the flesh" and the words *spirit* and *life* is that even though we are to literally eat/consume Jesus' flesh, as he commands in John 6, the value is primarily spiritual. In other words, we do not eat the Eucharist for bodily sustenance but for spiritual sustenance. In *The Bible Proves the Teachings of the Catholic Church*, Br. Peter Dimond explains that by emphasizing to his followers that his flesh and blood is "spirit and life," Jesus was dispelling their notion that all they should be concerned with is having flesh to eat to sustain life. The Eucharist is the actual flesh and blood of Jesus, as well as his soul and divinity, but it primarily brings about spiritual endowment. It is primarily for the sustenance of spiritual life.

The more likely meaning of these words is that Jesus is calling upon the disciples to be more spiritual in their thinking of this matter and less like men (flesh). The words that Jesus had spoken throughout the Bread of Life Discourse are of spirit and life because they indeed come from above and sustain life.

JOHN 6:60 "THIS SAYING IS HARD"

Perhaps the best evidence that Jesus was speaking literally—that he meant exactly what he said—comes from two of the concluding verses in John 6.

Then many of his disciples who were listening said, "This saying is hard; who can accept it?"....As a result of this, many [of] his disciples returned to their former way of life and no longer accompanied him.

John 6:60, 66

If Jesus had been speaking metaphorically, it seems reasonable that he would have tried to stop this group of potentially thousands from leaving him by saying he was speaking symbolically. Wouldn't he have said something like, "Wait! You misunderstand. What I mean by eating my flesh is...." The only thing that makes sense is that he let them walk away because there was *no* misunderstanding. Jesus meant exactly what he said.

It's noteworthy that those disgruntled people who did an about-face were not casual followers. As John 6:66 states, these were his "disciples," people who had already given up much to follow him. They were the same disciples present in the crowd of more than 5,000 who the day prior had witnessed the miracle of the loaves and who wanted to carry Jesus off and make him king.

While we can understand the complex feelings and a myriad of questions many of the disciples encountered in hearing Christ's message, remember that everything Jesus taught—most especially about the Eucharist—was intended for all times and all generations, not just for those in the large crowd that day. Furthermore, Jesus made a point throughout his ministry to explain to his disciples what his parables meant. On this topic, *Credo Ecclesiam unam, sanctam, catholicam et apostolicam* states:

> Does Jesus have an obligation to explain Himself to disciples? While parables are symbolic language often used by our Lord when He deals with the public or unbelieving, corrupt leadership, we see that Jesus does in fact explain the meaning behind his parables to his disciples privately. We see this with the Parable of the Wheat and Tares in Matthew 13 ("Then he left the crowd and went into the house. His disciples came to him and said, 'Explain to us the parable of the weeds in the field'") and again in Matthew 20:17 when our Lord took the twelve apart privately and explained to them the details of what He had been prophesying about his Passion. So, while allowing unbelievers to walk away confused is plausible, our Lord never sends the disciples away confused. He always takes care that they at least understand his words in the proper sense, and in John 6 He allows them to believe his words to be literal. They may not understand the words at the time (hence Peter's confused but faithful utterance, "You alone have the words of eternal life" in John 6:68), but they believe him nonetheless.

Had we been with Jesus, we might hope our response to him would have been like Peter's. While this teaching was difficult to understand, remember: "What is impossible for human beings is possible for God" (Luke 18:27).

Thankfully, this teaching and the fragrance of its grace that lies in its wake remains for us to study and learn from. Hopefully, it is enough for you to draw an informed conclusion: Jesus meant what he said. And if he meant what he said, then we must know and react accordingly to the fact that he comes to us substantially at every Mass, to pour out his amazing grace.

Whether this is clear to you yet or not, there is so much more to explore in this first leg of our relay race. The next three legs build off of Jesus' teaching in John 6. One that particularly stems directly from the Bread of Life Discourse is the Last Supper.

THE LAST SUPPER

What seems to some to have been an unacceptable, difficult-to-understand teaching in Capernaum reemerges and takes center stage at the Last Supper. It was so important that Jesus brings it forward on the night of his passion and death. Given the timing, and the fact that the Last Supper events are recorded in five New Testament writings (Matthew 26, Mark 14, Luke 22, John 13—17, 1 Corinthians 11), Jesus' words and their meaning cannot be underscored enough.

The key to understanding Jesus' words and actions at the Last Supper lies in several things: their connection to the Bread of Life Discourse; all of the Old Testament eucharistic prefigurements discussed earlier; and the framework presented in the question of whether or not Jesus is speaking literally or symbolically.

The Protestant view is that Jesus is saying, "Do this in memory [or remembrance] of me" as a call to a simple Christian ritual reenactment designed to forever remember the start of his passion. For Protestants, it is not Jesus giving a perpetual gift of grace: his entire self—his Body, Blood, soul, and divinity to his faithful.

Their argument against the Catholic view lies in how New Testament accounts are to be understood. Their view hinges on the explanation that Jesus was speaking metaphorically when he said "this is my body" and "this is my blood." And proof of this lies in the fact that Jesus tells his apostles to do this in remembrance of him as a simple memorial of the start of his passion. Is "this is my body" a metaphor or literal?

I came across a Protestant translation of the Bible, *The Amplified Bible* (*AMP*), that I wasn't previously familiar with. Based largely on the *American Standard* translation (*ASV*), the *AMP* version is designed to "amplify" the text by adding words and punctuation that are not found in the *ASV* translation. The goal of these additions is to give the reader a clearer understanding of the context behind the Protestant interpretation. Within their representation of 1 Corinthians 11:24, the larger evangelical, metaphoric interpretation of "this is my body" becomes evident: "And when He had given thanks, He broke it and said, "This is [represents] My body, which is [offered as a sacrifice] for you. Do this in [affectionate] remembrance of Me."

All four New Testament accounts of the Last Supper quote Jesus as saying the same four words as he held the bread in his hand: "This is my body." And when he held the cup in his hands, he says either, "This is my blood," or, "the new covenant in my blood." With these words, was Jesus speaking of a "representation" of his body and blood, as the *AMP* interpretation wants to depict?

The fact that each New Testament record of the Last Supper reports Jesus saying "this is my body"—and not "this is a *symbol* of my body"—is evidence in itself that he means exactly what he is saying, just as he did in John 6. But let's also consider that all three Gospel accounts use the same Greek phrase to say this is my body and this is my blood: "*Touto estin to some mou*," which translates to "this is actually my body" or "this is really my body." Paul's writing on the event is quite similar: "*Touto mou estin to soma*" and translates pretty much the same.

An article on Catholic.com on the institution of the Mass cites that the key to understanding what Jesus meant in his use of these words lies within the translation of the Greek verb *estin*, which is the equivalent of the English word *is*. It can mean "is really" or "is figuratively." According to the study of Greek grammar, the usual meaning of estin is the former. Similarly in English, "is" ascribes a literal understanding. Some fundamentalists explain the usage of "is" under the premise that Syriac (derived from the Aramaic alphabet)—the language Christ spoke—didn't have a word for "represents." But Nicholas Cardinal Wiseman, author of *The Real Presence of the Body and Blood of Our Lord Jesus Christ in the Blessed Eucharist, Proved from Scripture in Eight Lectures* (1859), showed that Aramaic has dozens of words that relay the meaning "represents."

Further support for the literal translation of Christ's words at the Last Supper come from St. Paul: "The cup of blessing that we bless, is it not a participation in the blood of Christ? The bread that we break, is it not a participation in the body of Christ?" (1 Corinthians 10:16).

The passage is clear. It is actually participating in the Body and Blood of Christ and not just eating symbolically of them. Paul also said, "Therefore whoever eats the bread and drinks the cup of the Lord unworthily will have to answer for the body and blood of the Lord....For anyone who eats and drinks without discerning the body, eats and drinks judgment on himself" (1 Corinthians 11:27, 29). If eating his Body and drinking his Blood unworthily is tantamount to committing a serious crime, it doesn't make sense that the action is symbolic in nature.

Catholics have come to understand that to receive the Eucharist unworthily, that is to say while in a state of grave sin, is in itself a grave and serious matter. Paul's assertion that to participate in the earliest celebrations of the Eucharist unworthily would bring judgment upon an individual only makes sense if we are participating in something much greater than a symbol.

THE PASSOVER CONNECTION

A final validation for a literal translation for "this is my body" and "this is my blood" comes from the connection we made earlier to the Passover. The Last Supper was a Passover meal celebrated by Jesus and the apostles. A Jewish Passover meal centers upon the body and blood of the lamb that was sacrificed earlier in the day. During this sacrifice, the blood from all the lambs slaughtered that day (estimated to be 200,000) was taken by the priests of the Temple and thrown onto the base of the altar, thereby atoning for the sins of the people.

As Brandt Pitre notes in *Jesus and the Jewish Roots of the Eucharist*, the Last Supper was no ordinary Passover meal:

> Jesus not only kept the Jewish Passover, he also deliberately altered it, thereby instituting a new Passover. As a Jewish man, he had celebrated Passover many times before; he knew full well what he was doing by changing it this time. He was showing that this was no ordinary Passover; it was the Passover of the Messiah, the night on which some Jews believed that

Israel would be "redeemed" (Exodus Rabbah 18:11). That is why Jesus can say his blood—not the blood of the Passover lamb—will be poured out for the forgiveness of sins.

Pitre continues: "By means of his words over the bread and wine of the Last Supper, Jesus is saying in no uncertain terms, 'I am the new Passover Lamb of the new exodus. This is the Passover of the Messiah, and I am the new sacrifice.'" As Pitre notes, Jesus is leading this Passover meal, but he is also the sacrifice being offered...he is both priest and lamb.

One more crucial thing points to a literal interpretation of "this is my body." For a Passover meal to be completed, the lamb has to be consumed in its entirety. Jesus is the lamb of the new Passover: he must be consumed. In participating in the Eucharist, we do just that. Within this fact lies the certainty that, just like in John 6, Jesus' words at the Last Supper mean our path to life lies in his life-giving flesh.

DO THIS IN REMEMBRANCE OF ME

Even with everything presented, the evangelical view may still counter the assertion that Jesus was speaking literally about his Body and Blood at the Last Supper. The evangelical view contends that Christians are being asked to simply participate in a memory of that evening and the passion to follow. But this is no mere memory, something that happened in the past that remains in the past. In fact, during the time of Christ, for the Jewish people to remember something meant more than recalling and reminiscing about it. To remember something was to make that past moment present again.

Pitre also speaks to this by explaining the Passover was not just a sacrifice but also a "memorial" or "remembrance" (see Exodus 12:14).

Jewish people would somehow "make present" the deliverance that had been won for their ancestors in the exodus from Egypt. As time passed, the elements of both remembrance and presence came to be expressed in a variety of rituals. In other words, ancient Jewish celebrants did not just remember the exodus; they actively participated in it.

Amazingly, this is what the Church teaches regarding the sacrifice of the Mass. Contrary to Protestant misunderstanding, Catholics do not resacrifice Jesus during the Mass, we do not reenact Calvary or recrucify our Lord. That sacrifice was once and for all when it occurred. We do just as the Jews of Jesus' time did with the Exodus through the Passover: we make that sacrifice present again and actively participate within it. The sacrifice of the Mass and the Eucharist is in no way a simple remembrance of the past, it makes present its reality. It makes present, per his love and direction, Jesus Christ himself.

THE OUR FATHER

With the baton still firmly in the hand of Jesus, we now enter into the final "meters" of the first leg of our relay race. As already discovered, the earliest Greek translation of the New Testament proves extremely useful in coming to understand what those authors intended to express in their writings. Such an examination of the Our Father leads to a discovery of a solitary Greek word with amazing eucharistic implications. That single word is *epiousios*.

Since the Eucharist is bread-centric, it's right to assume that *epiousios* makes its appearance within the line of the Our Father that reads, "Give us this day our daily bread." The backstory of this word's origin is highly intriguing. *Epiousios* appears only two times in the entire Bible. Both are within the same line of the Our Father and are found in Matthew 6:11 and in Luke 11:3. Additionally, it also appears in two other known texts: a fifth-century Egyptian papyrus and the *Didache*. Of further interest is that *epiousios* is what linguists call a *hapax legomenon*, which is a word or phrase that appears only once in a manuscript, document, or particular area of literature. Catholic Online affirms our understanding: "the word *epiousios* is...a *hapax legomenon*, an invented word that fills a unique need."

Epiousios is an adjective that modifies the word "bread," as in "give us this day our daily bread." In both scriptural references, it is being used in the place of the word commonly used for "daily." Since it is a curated word used to describe something that existing words can't, the best way to grasp the meaning is to break it into its constitutive parts. Derived from two Greek words, *Epi* is best translated as "above" or "super," and *ousios* as "substance." Since *epiousios* modifies the word for bread, the translation for this line of the Our Father becomes, "Give us this day our 'supersubstantial' bread."

The fact that this word appears in the earliest written record of the Bible and almost nowhere else in all of literature is worth contemplation. When we join the superlative use of *epiousios* to everything else we have studied regarding the role of bread throughout salvation history, including Manna, Showbread, the Multiplication of Loaves, the Bread of Life Discourse, and the Last Supper, is it even reasonable to consider its connection to the Eucharist is a matter of mere coincidence?

Understanding that there may be a few questions on the interpretation of *epiousios*, let us take an even deeper dive into the matter. Here is how Matthew 6:11 reads in Greek: Τὸν ἄρτον ἡμῶν τὸν ἐπιούσιον δὸς ἡμῖν σήμερον.

Of interest to us are the words ἄρτον (bread), ἐπιούσιον (*epiousios*—supersubstantial), and σήμερον (today). Contained here, from the earliest Greek translation of the Bible, are the three key words that lead to a literal translation of "give us this day our supersubstantial bread." So important is the bread Jesus is describing here that the word for "daily" needed modification to a word that had to be created in order to accurately convey what Jesus had said in his Aramaic tongue!

Recall in the section of the Bread of Life Discourse the unusual use of the word *trogon* for eat, versus the tremendously more common *phago*. Think back as well about how trogon's use brought with it a special attention and how it added high definition to the message that Jesus was conveying.

We have the same kind of dynamic happening here within the Our Father. Rather than going with the common Greek word for daily: *hemera*, the highly skilled translators of the early Greek books of the New Testament instead use a hapax legomenon, a word so rare that it is found in only three known texts throughout history. It is reasonable to consider that through the unique use of *epiousios* (supersubstantial), as opposed to the common use of *hemera* (daily), Jesus purposefully gave an enhanced meaning to the bread he speaks about in the Our Father.

To put in perspective how unique a choice of *epiousios* was for Greek translators, a few phrases showing examples of the wide use of *hemera* within the New Testament follow:

Matthew 20:2 "after agreeing with them for the usual daily wage"

Luke 9:23 "and take up his cross daily"

Acts 6:1 "their widows were being neglected in the daily distribution"

Acts 17:11 "and examined the scriptures daily"

Acts 17:17 "and daily in the public square"

Acts 19:9 "and began to hold daily discussions"

2 Corinthians 11:28 "There is the daily pressure"

Hebrews 3:13 "Encourage yourselves daily"

Hebrews 10:11 "Every priest stands daily at his ministry"

Throughout the years, there has been some debate on how *epiousios* is best translated. In the year 383, St. Jerome completed his translation of the Greek Old and New Testaments to Latin. In his work, St. Jerome translated *epiousios* in two different ways. For Matthew 6:11, he stuck with supersubstantial by going with the Latin word *supersubstantialem*. But when he translated the same part of the Our Father found in Luke 11:3, he instead went with the Latin word for daily, *quotidianum*.

Scholar Ryan Hanning, PhD, professor of theology and a fellow at the Institute of Catholic Theology, gives insight on the difference in St. Jerome's two translations. He thinks the word use selected by Jerome (and other scholars as well) in Matthew was meant to point out the characteristics of the infinite quality of the "Bread of Life." That is, highlight the spiritual and future anticipation of God's spiritual providence. The word used in Luke was meant to point out the sufficient quantity of "daily bread," that is, to highlight God's providence. This view doesn't solve the primary issue but acknowledges that both characteristics of the spiritual and practical understanding of bread are reflected.

Regardless of any debate on its translation, the fact that *epiousios* was applied versus *hemeran* in the earliest compilation of the Bible remains meaningful. Adding greater significance is that St. Jerome still retained this spiritual meaning in his translation of Matthew 6:11.

The appearance of *epiousios* in the earliest Church liturgical manual, the *Didache* further solidifies the significance of "our supersubstantial bread." The *Didache* dates back to the years 90–110 and was written in Greek. It was written on the heels of the writings of the New Testament and the lives of the apostles. In section 8:2 of this text, we get a translation of the Our Father that mirrors the wording found in Matthew 6:11. Of particular interest is that it uses *epiousios* for "daily," rather than the more common *hemeran*.

Further support for *epiousios* comes from one of the first Bibles to translate St. Jerome's Latin Vulgate to English: the *Douay-Rheims Bible*, around 1582. The main purpose for the publication was to uphold Catholic Tradition in the face of the emerging Protestant Reformation. As such, a primary goal was to translate the Bible in a literal and accurate manner from the Latin Vulgate as possible. In their translation of St. Jerome's Latin Bible to English, *Douay-Rheims* still translates Matthew 6:11 as "give us this day our supersubstantial bread."

When you then combine this fact with all the other prefigurements of bread and the entirety of John 6, it should become quite difficult to conclude that Jesus was speaking of just ordinary bread. Rather, when we pray "Give us this day our daily bread" in the Our Father, we should be praying not for ordinary bread but for the Bread of Life: the Body, Blood, soul, and divinity of Jesus Christ himself.

LEG ONE: CLOSING THOUGHTS

If you started leg one of our relay race as either a Protestant or Catholic doubter of Christ's True Presence in the Eucharist, remember, at one time I was right there with you. I was the artistic director of my children's "I Remember" Communion banners. The one who sat them down and lectured (to a seven-year-old) the symbolic nature of the Eucharist. So trust me, I understand where you are coming from. Everything laid out in this chapter is what began to shift my understanding away from this symbolic belief to the certainty that in the Eucharist, Jesus Christ stands in his completion. When examined thoroughly, it is hard to take these teachings of Jesus any other way than literally. If you picked up this book as a skeptic, I hope you are beginning to feel a spark of belief as a result of these teachings. And if you've been a consistent believer in the Real Presence, I hope what has been presented helps to strengthen and deepen your belief.

Let's move on to bring further clarity and understanding to the true nature of the Eucharist. At this point, Jesus hands off the relay baton directly to his immediate followers by sharing his teachings. In the manner in which Jesus' teachings are upheld and taught by his disciples in their entirety—without contradiction, addition, or subtraction—our belief in the Eucharist becomes further strengthened.

In the second leg of our relay race, we investigate the uniformity in which the immediate followers of Jesus taught and brought forward his gift of the Eucharist.

Remember, one of the purposes of this book is to provide an easy and succinct way to share the truth about the Eucharist with others. While you may have your doubts about being able to accomplish this after reading all that was presented in this chapter, stick with it. Toward the end, you will be given the tools to easily summarize the basic content packed into leg one.

CHAPTER 5

Leg Two:
The Teachings
of the Apostles

Without question, the most critical component of the meaning of the Eucharist lies within what Jesus himself taught. Nevertheless, how that teaching carries forward in time can lend either credibility or doubt to that original teaching. If the teaching becomes diluted or altered from its foundation, it could become easier to believe less in the original instruction. However, if the message adheres to the original, then it becomes easier to validate and believe all aspects, including the origin of that message.

With our relay baton being handed from Jesus to his direct followers, let's now take a look at what the New Testament writers said about the Eucharist. We will also examine how closely their teachings match what Jesus himself taught.

LEG TWO

My previous chapter related some of the quintessential eucharistic New Testament writings, chiefly John 6. Since the quotations of Jesus himself are in that chapter, they stand alone as validation of Jesus' literal claims about his Real Presence in the Eucharist.

An article titled "The Eucharist" on ScriptureCatholic. com, a resource on teachings of the Catholic faith, lists more than 125 New Testament verses linked to the Eucharist. Admittedly, many of those hundred-plus verses are theologically related to the Eucharist, as opposed to being direct, clear teachings about it. Still, a great many connective references to both the theology and the practices of the sacrament can be found within the New Testament.

Certainly, touching on each of those verses with a connection to the Eucharist would be laborious and redundant. Instead, this chapter focuses on New Testament writings that best demonstrate the amazing permanence to the teachings of Jesus. In particular, we focus here on the writings of Paul, the Acts of the Apostles, and the Book of Revelation.

THE WRITINGS OF PAUL

Christians of all denominations regard Paul as one of the greatest apostles, even though he was not among the original twelve. He is of interest in this book for many reasons, primarily because of the number of writings he produced, including his letters to various early churches. Paul wrote thirteen of the twenty-seven New Testament books. Calculated on a per-word basis, his writings represent about 28 percent of the New Testament, depending on the Bible version examined.

Paul's writings are important because they represent the earliest works about the life of Jesus. As a case in point, a pivotal writing by Paul on the Eucharist is found in 1 Corinthians, a letter probably written between the years 53 and 54.

The Jerome Biblical Commentary—a contemporary verse-by-verse look at the scientific, literary, and historical content of the Scriptures—says Corinthians is likely the earliest extant testimony about the institution of the Eucharist. According to this commentary, First Corinthians, written about twenty years after Christ's ascension and eight years before Mark's Gospel, gives access to the earliest teachings, beliefs, and practices of the early Church, most specifically to the Eucharist.

Paul's texts on the Eucharist are consistent with Jesus' own teaching, that Christ is truly present in the Eucharist. Four key Pauline works illustrate this point.

1 CORINTHIANS 11:23–25

In the previous chapter's discussion on the Last Supper, I examined the Gospel accounts of it and Paul's text:

> For I received from the Lord what I also handed on to you, that the Lord Jesus, on the night he was handed over, took bread, and, after he had given thanks, broke it and said, "This is my body that is for you. Do this in remembrance of me." In the same way also the cup, after supper, saying, "This cup is the new covenant in my blood. Do this, as often as you drink it, in remembrance of me."
>
> *1 Corinthians 11:23–25*

Again, the Greek translation for "this is my body" is "*touto mou estin to soma,*" meaning "this is really my body." The key to understanding what Jesus meant in his use of these words lies within the translation of the Greek verb *estin,* translating to "is" or "is really," not to "represents."

In Jesus' native tongue there are roughly three dozen words for "represents." Greek translators of the early books of the New Testament use *estin* likely because Paul did. If Paul, who wrote in Greek, had used any of the many available words for "represents" or "symbolizes," that word likely would have been clearly translated as he intended. So the use of *estin* in the earliest transcripts of 1 Corinthians favors the belief that Jesus was speaking literally when he said, "This is my body."

Also remember, for the Jews during the time of Christ, "to remember" was to make an event present once again. This happens at every Mass: Christ is made fully present. So when Jesus says, "Do this in remembrance of me," he is speaking of far more than a simple memorial of a past event.

Since Paul writes so soon after the life of Christ, his intentional use of "this is my body" demonstrates that the early Church indeed believed that at the breaking of the bread they were encountering the Real Presence of Christ.

1 CORINTHIANS 11:26–29

Immediately following Paul's description of the Last Supper, he delivers two strong proclamations. "For as often as you eat this bread and drink the cup, you proclaim the death of the Lord until he comes" (1 Corinthians 11:26). In this verse, Paul brings the Eucharist together into the three dimensions of time: in reference to Jesus' death (past), in the call for Jesus' followers to repeat this rite as long as history lasts (present), and until Jesus' return to humanity (future).

This convergence of time within the context of the Lord's Supper reveals a depth unlikely for a simple memorial. But what Paul says next provides the strongest reasons for us to believe that Paul taught the Real Presence of Christ:

> Therefore, whoever eats the bread or drinks the cup of the Lord unworthily will have to answer for the body and blood of the Lord. A person should examine himself, and so eat the bread and drink the cup. For anyone who eats and drinks without discerning the body, eats and drinks judgment on himself.
>
> *1 Corinthians 11:27–29*

If Paul was teaching that the Eucharist was just a symbolic memorial, then does it make sense that before receiving the bread and wine of the Lord's Supper that partakers would first have to undergo a self-examination? Unlikely. Perplexing as well would be the requirement for people to have judgment cast upon himself or herself if they were to receive the Eucharist in a state of serious sin.

Catholics can probably relate to Paul's words and how they tie into the Church's practices today about receipt of holy Communion. For Protestants and others who may not be familiar with Catholic customs, I offer an explanation.

Since Catholics believe in the literal teaching of Christ regarding his complete, total, Real Presence in the Eucharist, we believe we must be free from serious sin (in a state of grace) in order to worthily receive Christ in the Eucharist. Thus before the celebration of the Eucharist at Mass, we take time to examine our conscience. Through thoughtful introspection, we determine if there is any serious sin that we have committed that requires reconciliation. If there is, we cannot receive holy Communion until that reconciliation with God, through the sacrament of reconciliation, occurs. In fact, to knowingly receive the Eucharist while in a serious state of sin is a grave sin itself.

A final consideration in unearthing the meaning of Paul's teaching lies in the last sentence of those verses: "For anyone who eats and drinks without discerning the body, eats and drinks judgment on himself." Not only do people drink judgment upon themselves for receiving the Eucharist in a state of sin, they also do so if they do not "discern the body of Christ." A symbolic action requires simple participation. The enormities involved in the reality of Jesus Christ giving us himself—his Body, Blood, soul, and divinity—requires more than mere participation. It requires a belief that must be discerned. That's why when Catholics are presented the Eucharist at Mass and the priest says, "This is my body," we contemplate that truth and affirm aloud, "Amen," meaning, "yes, we believe this is really Christ!" Or as our good friend Thomas the Apostle might say, "My Lord and my God!"

1 CORINTHIANS 10:15-18

I am speaking as to sensible people; judge for yourselves what [I say]. The cup of blessing that we bless, is it not a participation in the blood of Christ? The bread that we break, is it not a participation in the body of Christ? Because the loaf of bread is one, we, though many, are one body, for we all partake of the one loaf. Look at Israel according to the flesh; are not those who eat the sacrifices participants in the altar?

1 Corinthians 10:15–18

These verses from Paul to the Church at Corinth demonstrate these connections to the Eucharist:

- The participation, in the cup, in the Blood of Christ.
- The bread and cup/Body and Blood that we partake in makes us one.

PARTICIPATION IN THE CUP

Paul's reference to the cup should sound familiar, as it connects to Jesus' institution of the Eucharist at the Last Supper. Recall verse 11:25 of this same letter, where Paul quotes Jesus as saying, "This cup is the new covenant in my blood" (1 Corinthians 11:25). The Cup of Blessing Paul speaks of here is the Passover Cup of Blessing that Jesus transformed into the eucharistic cup of the New Covenant at the Last Supper. And what is contained in the cup? Paul writes that it is the "blood" of Christ. Not a metaphor, not a symbol thereof.

As for the word *participation* that Paul uses here and elsewhere, the *Ignatius Catholic Study Bible* says: "Eucharistic Communion [participation] unites believers with Christ and one another. These two blessings are related inasmuch as the Sacrament of Christ's Body and Blood is what continues to mold us into the ecclesial body of Christ, the Church."

THE BREAD AND WINE/BODY AND BLOOD MAKE US ONE

As with the cup that we "participate" in, Paul writes that the one loaf which we "partake" of makes us, though many, one. How can ordinary bread or wine make us one? Within human boundaries, this is implausible. But as the quote describes, this is not ordinary bread and wine. It is Christ himself, so it becomes easy to understand how participation in this meal truly makes us one Church in Christ.

PARTICIPANTS IN THE ALTAR

The final line of these verses from 1 Corinthians is of particular interest: "Are not those who eat the sacrifices participants in the altar?"

That quotation refers to the eating of the new Lamb of the Passover, Christ. More so, he is the Lamb of God, the sacrificial lamb God gave to atone for our sins once and for all. Recall that a key requirement of the Passover meal was that the lamb had to be completely consumed. We are called to enter into the sacrifice. Through the priesthood, the sacrifice of Calvary is made present to us at every Mass. Everything happening at the altar makes present the Last Supper, the new Passover. Thus, we can only participate fully if we consume the Lamb, Jesus, the sacrifice of God himself. The *Catechism* soundly connects Christ's sacrifice and the altar when it states:

> The altar, around which the Church is gathered in the celebration of the Eucharist, represents the two aspects of the same mystery: the altar of the sacrifice and the table of the Lord. This is all the more so since the Christian altar is the symbol of Christ himself, present in the midst of the assembly of his faithful, both as the victim offered for our reconciliation and as food from heaven who is giving himself to us. "For what is the altar of Christ if not the image of the Body of Christ?" asks St. Ambrose. He says elsewhere, "The altar represents the Body [of Christ] and the Body of Christ is on the altar." The liturgy expresses this unity of sacrifice and communion in many prayers.
>
> *CCC* 1383

This is the tie that binds when we participate at the altar, given in the love and wisdom of God. Aware of this, Paul passes on this understanding to the early Church faithful.

BREAKING OF THE BREAD EQUALS
THE EUCHARISTIC CELEBRATION

"The bread that we break, is it not a participation in the body of Christ?" This second part of verse 16 is significant. First, a common term for the earliest eucharistic celebration of the Church is the "breaking of the bread." The eucharistic celebration is, to this day, often referred to as the "breaking of the bread." Evangelicals generally argue that when the breaking of the bread is mentioned in the New Testament, it signifies a simple common communal meal and not a sacramental receiving of the Lord's Body, Blood, soul, and divinity. My internet search of some non-Catholic links about the breaking of the bread uncovered nothing about Catholic beliefs.

One example from the United Church reads, "Breaking bread simply meant sharing a normal meal, the phrase coming from observation that a meal officially began when someone had broken off a piece of bread."

This explanation falls short when we consider Paul's words that clearly connect the bread they are breaking to "a participation in the body of Christ." If we believe Paul's account of the Last Supper from 1 Corinthians 11:23–25, "This is (*estin*) my body," then it follows that references made to the breaking of the bread are undeniably reflecting the early Church's practice and belief in the sacrament of holy Communion. On the meaning of the "breaking of the bread," the *CCC* teaches:

> The Breaking of Bread, because Jesus used this rite, part of a Jewish meal when as master of the table he blessed and distributed the bread, above all at the Last Supper. It is by this action that his disciples will recognize him after his Resurrection, and it is this expression that the first Christians will use to designate their Eucharistic assemblies; by doing so they signified that all who eat the one broken bread, Christ, enter into communion with him and form but one body in him.
>
> *CCC* 1329

Equating the "breaking of the bread" to the eucharistic reality shared by Catholics will become increasingly important when we look at passages in the Acts of the Apostles.

1 CORINTHIANS 10:21

> You cannot drink the cup of the Lord and also the cup of demons. You cannot partake of the table of the Lord and of the table of demons.
>
> *1 Corinthians 10:21*

In this verse, Paul addresses idolatry. You cannot participate in the eucharistic cup and be involved in any pagan practice, just like you can't receive holy Communion in a state of serious sin. Certainly, involvement with any pagan rituals or practices would qualify as serious sin, as it breaks the commandment, "...You shall not have strange gods before me."

If Communion was just bread and wine, how and why would Paul place such restrictions on its reception? Clearly Paul believes what he taught to the earliest Church: the reality of Christ's Real Presence in the holy Eucharist. He further invites the faithful to participate in the new Passover, and through it, the sacrifice of Calvary. If this sounds familiar, it should. These are the teachings of Jesus, handed down to the faithful without change.

While Paul's writings further strengthen the belief that Jesus is truly and fully present in the Eucharist, his is not the only record we have about the perpetuation of Jesus' institution of the sacrament of holy Communion. We turn now to the Acts of the Apostles for further revelations about the continuation of Jesus' most grace-filled sacrament.

THE ACTS OF THE APOSTLES

The Gospel evangelist Luke wrote the Book of the Acts of the Apostles. A physician and learned man, Luke took on the role of meticulous historian when he wrote Acts. His goal was to put forward an accurate account of Christ's life and the early

Church. To accomplish this, he interviewed a great number of people who were at the events he was recording. Likely written about the year 63, Luke's detailed work gives readers a front-row seat into the acts and mission of the early Church.

Like Paul, Luke identifies the practice of the Eucharist as the "breaking of the bread." Three times within Acts, he describes the faithful participating in the "breaking of the bread." As outlined in the previous section, there is little doubt that the early Church's reference to the breaking of the bread meant Christ becoming fully present in the Eucharist.

The Breaking of the Bread in the Acts of the Apostles (Acts 2:42, Acts 2:46, Acts 20:7)

One of the first events in the Book of Acts is Peter's passionate and Holy Spirit-led post-Pentecost speech to Jerusalem. What he said was so impactful, Luke records in Acts 2:41, that more than 3,000 people accepted his message and were baptized. Next he describes the daily activities—the "mission"—of the early Church:

> They devoted themselves to the teaching of the apostles and to the communal life, to the breaking of the bread and to the prayers.
>
> *Acts 2:42*

This verse states activities that would be expected of this new group of believers. Since Christ's actions presented an addition to their Jewish identity, being devoted to the teachings of those who were closest to Christ makes more than great sense. It would be essential! Another vital component to this emerging community is listed: prayer.

Between teaching and praying, Luke recounts that these new followers of Christ devoted themselves to the communal life and to the breaking of the bread. Since a huge part of living in "communal life" with one another involves meals, it would seem unnecessary for Luke to include the "breaking of the bread" if it referred to a meal. Here, "breaking of the bread" appears to be something in addition to a shared meal within a community. For this reason, a more plausible conclusion would be that it is a direct reference to a sacred rite, the Eucharist. In his article "The Church of the Apostles," esteemed author Kenneth D. Whitehead furthers this understanding in his comments related to Acts 2:42:

> These first Christians "devoted themselves to the apostles' teaching and fellowship, to the breaking of the bread and the prayers" (Acts 2:42). We should take careful note of this brief description of the activities of the early Christians. We can deduce from it that the Christians who first adopted the faith of Jesus Christ under the headship of Peter and the other apostles subscribed to a specific doctrine about what they must believe and do in order to be saved ("the apostles' teaching") belonged to a definite, organized

community ("the Church"), which was precisely the one led by the same apostles ("the apostles'...fellowship"), and participated in a sacred rite which included a meal that was regularly enacted ("the breaking of the bread").

In Luke's description of the life of the earliest Church, he mentions "breaking of the bread" a second time in Acts 2: "... They devoted themselves to meeting together in the temple area and to breaking bread in their homes" (Acts 2:46).

Since the early Church faithful saw their belief in Christ as a continuation of their Judaism, it makes sense that they still went to the temple. Likewise, since the eucharistic meal was not part of temple worship, that celebration was held in homes.

Renowned Catholic Scripture scholar Fr. Charles Jerome Callan supports the belief that the breaking of the bread equates to the eucharistic banquet in his commentary on Acts 2:42–47:

St. Luke in these verses describes the life and practices of the first Christians. According to the Vulgate, their occupations were threefold: (a) attendance at doctrine, (b) participation in the breaking of bread, (c) assistance at prayer. But from the Greek manuscript, we gather more than this, and find that their religious practices were: (a) to assist regularly at the instructions given by the apostles on the life and teachings of Jesus; (b) to take part in works of fraternal charity for the community of Christians, who were already living together, separate from the Jews; (c) to assist at the "celebration of the Eucharist" (as it is called in the Syriac version) and receive holy Communion (which was called " the breaking," i.e., the eating "of bread"); (d) to assist at "prayers," which were most likely recited in public at fixed hours.

See commentary by Fr. Charles Jerome Callen at: thedivinelamp.wordpress.com

The last "breaking bread" reference I will make comes from Acts 20 and gives us insight into the start of our current practice of worshiping on Sunday: "On the first day of the week when we gathered to break bread, Paul spoke to them because he was going to leave on the next day, and he kept on speaking until midnight" (Acts 20:7). The first day of the week for Jews of this time was the day after the Sabbath (the Sabbath was recognized on Saturday at this point in history). According to the *Ignatius Catholic Study Bible*, this verse is the earliest evidence that believers assembled on Sundays for catechetical instruction and sacramental worship: that is, the "breaking of the bread."

In Acts, Luke confirms that in its earliest stages the Church celebrated the Eucharist. We also learn that this participation took place on Sunday and involved prayers and teaching. Through these glimpses of the infant Church, we see the roots of what will become the Mass. Speaking of the Mass, we now turn our attention to the Bible book about the Mass: Revelation.

THE BOOK OF REVELATION

This book can be daunting for many. Leviathans, dragons, creatures with seven heads and ten horns, and most especially the mention of "the beast," may dissuade us from navigating our way through this last book of the Bible. Catholic convert and author Scott Hahn seems to agrees in a title he wrote to unveil the mysteries of the Mass, *The Lamb's Supper: The Mass as Heaven on Earth.* In it he speaks to the disturbing visuals presented in Revelation and the likelihood that "some Catholics" may be inclined to skip over a deep dive into this prophetic book. What Hahn discovers and discusses in his book is that Revelation holds very close ties to the liturgy and the celebration of the Mass.

Before going further into Revelation, it is in relay leg two because a consensus view holds that the authorship of it belongs to John the Apostle, the author of the Gospel of John. Why? The author identifies himself in the writing simply as "John," with no further explanation. The fact that the author merely states he is John, without any further specification, (like John of Tarsus, etc.) indicates that author John was so well-known at the time of Revelation's writing that only "John" is needed for identification.

John the Apostle's authorship of Revelation is also supported by the written testimony of several early Church Fathers, including St. Justin Martyr (year 165), St. Irenaeus (180), St. Clement of Alexandria (200), St. Hippolytus (225), and St. Athanasius (350).

The majority view of biblical scholarship is that Revelation was written around the year 90. This date comes close to the authorship testimonies of the early Church Fathers, lending meaningful credibility and support for John's authorship. Consider especially the fact that Justin Martyr and Irenaeus were writing just seventy-five to eighty years after John wrote Revelation. In historical terms, seventy-five to eighty years is a minuscule period of time.

Revelation's apostolic authorship assuredly enables it to fit into this chapter's exploration of what was taught and thought about the Eucharist in the Church in the immediate years after Jesus' ascension.

Revelation lends credibility to the early Church's belief in the Real Presence of Christ in the Eucharist because the book is filled with eucharistic descriptors, meaning, and purpose. Revelation is not a catechetical lesson plan on the Eucharist, nor is it a doctrine primer on what the Eucharist is, or a reference guide to Jesus' teachings on it. But perhaps more than any other book in the Bible, Revelation gives meaning to the sacrament.

The first step in understanding this is to realize the inseparable connection between the Eucharist and the Mass. Simply put—no Eucharist, no Mass. Thus, the Mass and Eucharist are synonymous, one and the same. We can have prayer or worship services without the Eucharist, but we cannot have the Mass without it.

With this background, we return to Hahn's book *The Lamb's Supper: The Mass as Heaven on Earth*. He relates his experience at his first Mass. At the time, he was a Protestant minister, a biblical scholar, and a theology professor. At Mass, he began taking in connections to everything he was seeing, hearing, and smelling, and recognized that everything in the Mass was linked directly to the Bible. Through his study of the Book of Revelation, he came to realize that what he saw happening before him at the Mass happened not only in that time and space but likewise in heaven at that moment.

Among everything else it is, the Book of Revelation is a tale of the eucharistic banquet in heaven. If the Mass cannot be separated from the Eucharist, nor the Eucharist from the Mass, then our last book of the Bible is overtly reminding us of the truth and utter importance of the Eucharist.

The Agape Catholic Bible Study website offers a chart to cross-reference various parts of the Mass with verses in Revelation as well as St. John's visions. Michael E. Hunt is the author of the resource "The Mass in the Vision of the Revelation of St. John" (AgapeBibleStudy.com, 1998, Revised 2007, used with permission). In the following table, note the number of connections to the Mass found in Revelation. Remember this. No Mass, no Eucharist. No Eucharist, no Mass.

Table 1

- Celebration of the Mass
- Introductory Rites
- Reference Verses in Revelation
- John's Vision in Revelation

Table 2

- Celebration of the Mass
- Liturgy of the Word
- Reference Verses in Revelation
- John's Vision in Revelation

Table 3

- Celebration of the Mass
- Liturgy of the Eucharist
- Reference Verses in Revelation
- John's Vision in Revelation

Celebration of the Mass *Introductory Rites*	Reference Verses in Revelation	John's Vision in Revelation
Sunday Worship	1:10	John's visions of heavenly worship on the Lord's day.
Processional: Presiding priest (in liturgical garment) and assisting ministers	1:6; 1:12–13; 4:4; 4:9–10; 5:6, 8–9, 14	Christ our High Priest in liturgical garment.

Celebration of the Mass *Liturgy of the Word*	Reference Verses in Revelation	John's Vision in Revelation
Entrance antiphon	4:8–11; 5:9–14; 7:10–12	Antiphonal chant
Priest reverences the altar, which represents the meeting place between man and God, by kissing the altar and with incense at a high or solemn Mass. He wears appropriate vestments.	6:9; 8:3–5; 9:13; 11:1; 14:18; 16:7 1:8; 4:2–3, 9; 5:1–13; 7:9–17; 19:4–9; 22:3–5 5:8; 8:3–5 1:12–13; 6:2, 11; 7:9, 14; 15:5–6; 19:8, 13–14; 4:2–3	Altar Worship in the presence of God Incense Liturgical vestments in the heavenly Sanctuary
Liturgical music, singing Celibate clergy	5:9, 11–12; 14:2–4; 15:3 14:4–5	Liturgical music, singing Consecrated celibacy
Sanctuary/tabernacle and presider's chair	11:19; 14:15; 15:5; 4:2–10; 5:1–14; 6:16; 7:9–17; 8:3; 12:5; 14:3–5; 19:4–5; 20:4; 21:3, 5; 22:1; 22:3;	Sanctuary/Tabernacle Throne in sanctuary
Baptismal, eucharistic, and altar candles	1:13; 2:5; 4:5	Lampstands (menorah)
Congregation of priesthood of believers	1:6; 19:7–9; 20:6	Priesthood of the faithful
Sign of the Cross, greeting	7:3; 14:1; 22:4	Sign of the Cross (mark of the Lamb)
Rite of Blessing	1:3; 14:13; 16:15; 19:9; 22:7, 14	Blessing
Penitential Act	Chapters 2 and 3	Penitence

Celebration of the Mass *Liturgy of the Word*	Reference Verses in Revelation	John's Vision in Revelation
Gloria Opening Prayer	15:3–4 4:11	Gloria Opening Prayer
Reading from the Word of God 1st reading: Old Testament Responsorial Psalms 2nd reading: New Testament	5:1–8; 10:8; 20:12 3:22 1:7 (ref. Daniel 7:13; Zechariah 12:10, 12) 12:1–2, 6, 13–14 12:5; 12:13–17	Book or scroll Messages from Christ References to Christ in Old Testament Virgin Mary, daughter of David, and Old Covenant; Mary, Mother of Christ and the Church
Alleluia and Gospel	19:1, 3, 4, 6 1:7 (John 19:34, 37)	Alleluia Gospel reference
Intercessions	5:8; 6:9–10; 8:3–4	Intercession of angels and saints
Eucharistic Host	2:17	Hidden manna
Preparation of gifts (wine in chalices, bread in bowls)	15:7; chapter 16 (in Revelation = judgments; in Mass = to become gifts of grace)	Bowls, chalices
Eucharistic Prayer and introductory dialogue = command, "Lift up your hearts."	11:12	Heavenly command: I heard a loud voice from heaven say to them, "Come up here."
Acclamation Holy, Holy, Holy (worshipers kneel after Sanctus)	4:8–10	Heavenly congregation sings "Holy, Holy, Holy," and worshipers kneel.

Celebration of the Mass *Liturgy of the Eucharist*	Reference Verses in Revelation	John's Vision in Revelation
The Great Amen Communion Rite	19:4; 22:21 5:1, 5–6	Great Amen; sacrificed Lamb in the sanctuary
Lamb of God, you take away the sins of the world.	Chapter 5, especially verse 6	Lamb of God
The Lamb of God takes away the sins of the world. Happy are those called to his table.	Chapter 19, especially verse 9	Marriage supper of the Lamb
Silent contemplation	8:1	Silent contemplation
Concluding Rites/ final blessing. The Mass of the Catholic Church is celebrated around the world.	22:7 7:9–17	Final blessing Worldwide worship Catholic (*katholikos* in Greek) means "universal"

This visual cross-reference reinforces the reality that the Mass on earth is in concert with the Mass in heaven.

Think back to the prefigurements of the Eucharist we discussed earlier. They started in Genesis with Melchizedek, the priest of Salem, offering bread and wine. That initial eucharistic thread weaves its way throughout the Bible, where it meets and ties together other eucharistic signs and teachings. When the thread gets to Revelation it becomes as thick as a rope. Revelation boldly reveals that the reality of the Eucharist is being proclaimed both on earth and in God's presence in heaven! Thus it makes no sense that the Eucharist, the Mass, would play such a central role in the last book of the Bible if it were merely a symbol and not the Lamb itself.

SUMMARY OF LEG TWO

As noted, there are more than 100 references made to the Eucharist in the New Testament from the followers of Jesus. While many are theologically tied and not direct statements, like "this is my body," the number of eucharistic connections coming from Jesus' followers after his death and resurrection is remarkable.

These life-giving teachings of Jesus remain unbroken and unaltered from Jesus' mouth to those of his closest followers. In our metaphoric language, the relay exchange between leg one and leg two of our race went perfectly.

We now turn to leg three of our relay race to see how the men who followed the apostles, the early Church Fathers, handled Jesus' teachings of the Eucharist.

CHAPTER 6

Leg Three:
The Teachings of the
Early Church Fathers

ollowing the earthly lives of the apostles, the most regarded teachers of the Christian faith were collectively known as the Church Fathers. Depending on the reference, about 100 men comprise those considered to be in this distinguished group. Beginning immediately after the apostles, the teaching authority of these individuals spanned into the eighth century, ending with the death of the last Church Father, St. John Damascus, in the year 749. Since we are most interested in seeing what happened to the teaching and practice of the Eucharist immediately after the apostles, our attention will focus on the writings of the earliest Church Fathers, those who wrote into the fourth century.

The writings of the early Church Fathers are richly significant because of their connection in time to the apostles. In his book *The Fathers of the Church*, author Mike Aquilina writes, "Their witness, (the early Church Fathers), is invaluable, because these Fathers were nearest to the Apostles, who were, in turn, nearest to Jesus."

One can see how Aquilina's statement runs parallel with our relay analogy. If a practice as significant as the Eucharist is to be held as true, then it ought to be able to be traced from the source of all Christian teaching—Jesus—forward to today, without distortion or interruption.

Before we turn to the writings of these early Church Fathers, we will first take a look at the previously mentioned *Didache*. While technically not authored by a Church Father, the *Didache*'s early date and wide acceptance lends substantial support to the recognition and celebration of the Eucharist by the Church immediately following the apostles.

THE *DIDACHE*

Didache, Greek for "teachings" or "the teachings," is formally known as *The Teachings of the Twelve Apostles*. While the author, or authors, are anonymous, dating of the *Didache* places its origin between the years 90 and 110. Biblical scholars lean to an early second-century dating for the document due to it being quoted in various second-century writings, including by the Church Father Clement of Alexandria.

The *Didache* has sixteen chapters and describes many practices, including several liturgical ones, of the early Church. Topics contained in these chapters include prayer, the rite of baptism, Church hierarchy, and, of course, the Eucharist. Of the sixteen chapters of the *Didache*, the Eucharist is detailed in two: Chapters nine and fourteen.

> Now concerning the Thanksgiving (Eucharist), thus give thanks. First concerning the cup: We thank you, our Father, for the holy vine of David Your servant, which You made known to us through Jesus Your Servant; to You be the glory forever. And concerning the broken bread: We thank You, our Father, for the life and knowledge which You made known to us through Jesus Your Servant; to You be the glory for-

ever. Even as this broken bread was scattered over the hills, and was gathered together and became one, so let Your Church be gathered together from the ends of the earth into Your kingdom; for Yours is the glory and the power through Jesus Christ forever. But let no one eat or drink of your Thanksgiving (Eucharist), but they who have been baptized into the name of the Lord; for concerning this also the Lord has said, Give not that which is holy to the dogs.

Matthew 7:6, Didache, chapter nine

The word *Eucharist* is presented four words into chapter nine of the *Didache*. While some translations of this word use *Thanksgiving* instead, thanksgiving is what the Greek word *Eucharist* means! In addition, some translations of this chapter actually use both words: "eucharistic thanksgiving."

The mere fact that the *Eucharist* is being used supports the idea that the Bread of Life being described is something vastly different than just two components of an ordinary meal. In addition, the reverent language being used in relationship to these items is deeply ritualistic, similar in kind to the prayers that Jesus said over these same items at the Last Supper.

The *Didache* was an early Church liturgical manual. It is possible that these words might represent the first designated prayers of eucharistic consecration used by the infant Mass. In fact, one translation of the first sentence of this chapter seems to particularly support this idea:

> And concerning the Thanksgiving (Eucharist), thus give thanks: First concerning the Cup.

The elevation of the Eucharist bread and cup is exactly what priests have done for centuries, and it continues today during the consecration of the Eucharist during the Mass.

If you still doubt that the *Didache* is not speaking directly of an early understanding of the Church of Christ's Real Presence in the Eucharist, the chapter's last words should help:

> But let no one eat or drink of your Thanksgiving (Eucharist), but they who have been baptized into the name of the Lord; for concerning this also the Lord has said, Give not that which is holy to the dogs.

Careful instruction is given in these lines as to who can and cannot receive the cup and bread. Only those who are baptized, who have entered into the Church in a formal way, are allowed to receive and participate in these revered gifts. The author punctuates this point by quoting Matthew 7:6, which also admonishes to "...not give what is holy to dogs."

If you were still believing that all previous references in Acts and by Paul to the "breaking of the bread" denoted nothing more than a simple communal meal, consider the use of the word "holy" in relationship to this bread and wine. While one would not typically use the word holy to describe the components of an ordinary meal, it does make sense if it were referring to the Real Presence of Christ.

> But every Lord's Day gather yourselves together, and break bread, and give thanksgiving after having confessed your transgressions, that your sacrifice may be pure. But let no one that is at variance with his fellow come together with you, until they be reconciled, that your sacrifice may not be profaned. For this is that which was spoken by the Lord: "In every place and time offer to me a pure sacrifice; for I am a great King, says the Lord, and my name is wonderful among the nations."
>
> *Didache,* chapter fourteen

Like chapter nine, *Didache* chapter fourteen makes clear that the bread being referred to is anything but ordinary. One of the things that stands out in these couple of sentences that supports the Eucharist being the Real Presence of Christ includes that this event is to occur on a special day, the Lord's Day (Sunday), a day set apart for the Lord.

A second more notable point is that in order to participate "in this Breaking of the Bread," people have to first confess their sins and fix any wrong done against a neighbor. This coincides with the Church's current practice about the worthy reception of the Eucharist. Today, as it was around the year 100, to take the Eucharist while in a state of serious sin is a grave act. It would make no sense for these restrictions to be in place if all that was involved during this meal was eating a simple piece of bread and taking a modest sip of wine.

The content of the *Didache*, coupled with its arrival at the time immediately following the Church leadership by the apostles, makes clear that what they had learned directly from Jesus regarding the Eucharist was not lost by the next generation. Quite the opposite. The *Didache* shows a refinement of these teachings and a deep and solemn reverence that had developed into a sacred liturgical practice.

We turn now from text by an anonymous writer to a group of men with traceable names and histories, who carry forward in their writings this same truth of the Eucharist and the Mass in which Christ's Real Presence is made manifest. Though a great number of writings on the Eucharist by the early Church Fathers exists, we will focus on five.

ST. IGNATIUS OF ANTIOCH

In my opinion, St. Ignatius plays a most critical and central role in demonstrating the reality of the Eucharist. Why? Saint Ignatius was a student and disciple of the Apostle John! Saint Ignatius' understanding of the Eucharist was formed by hearing directly from the author of both the Gospel of John and the Book of Revelation who also was at Jesus' side for three earthly years and for the forty days of his resurrected reign.

In our relay analogy, this is as close as it gets to a direct handoff from the apostles in leg two to the early Fathers in leg three of our race. All connect to leg one! Jesus teaches St. John, he teaches St. Ignatius, and he teaches the early faithful.

Remember, the Gospel of John is where, in chapter six, Jesus delivers the Bread of Life Discourse, his direct teachings of the Eucharist. If John, himself present at the Bread of Life Discourse, taught the reality of Christ's Presence in the Eucharist, then we should be inclined to believe it would be highlighted in the teachings of his student St. Ignatius.

The record of St. Ignatius is an inspiring one. After being schooled in all things Christ by John the Apostle, Ignatius served for more than four decades as the Bishop of Antioch. During the persecution of Trajan, St. Ignatius was captured and carried off to Rome where, by the eviscerating force of starved lions, he met his fate in the Coliseum in year 107.

During that journey from Antioch to Rome, Ignatius wrote seven letters that we have to this day, to the Churches in Asia Minor, Europe, Ephesus, Magnesia, Troas, Rome, Philadelphia, and Smyrna, and one to his friend Polycarp, the Bishop of Smyrna. Knowing his end was near, St. Ignatius wrote to these churches to testify to some of the key tenets of the early Christian Church. These topics included marriage, the Trinity, the Incarnation, the primacy of Rome, the authority of priests and bishops, and the Real Presence of Christ in the Eucharist.

We turn now to letters where St. Ignatius discusses the Real Presence of Christ in the Eucharist: his letters to the Romans and the Smyrnaeans.

St. Ignatius' Letter to the Romans 7:3

> I have no delight in corruptible food nor in the pleasures of this life. I desire the bread of God, the heavenly bread, the bread of life, which is the flesh of Jesus Christ, the Son of God, who became afterwards of the seed of David and Abraham; and I desire the drink of God, namely His blood, which is incorruptible love and eternal life.

Not only did St. Ignatius express beliefs in keeping with the writings of the *Didache*, a document written during the same time period, but it is also consistent with the teachings of Jesus in John 6. As bold and as clearly as can be stated, we hear St. Ignatius echo the words of Jesus himself...that the bread, the Eucharist is the Body of Christ and the drink is his Blood.

St. Ignatius' Letter to the Smyrnaeans 6:2–7:1

> But consider those who are of a different opinion with respect to the grace of Christ which has come unto us, how opposed they are to the will of God. They have no regard for love; no care for the widow,

or the orphan, or the oppressed; of the bond, or of the free; of the hungry, or of the thirsty. They abstain from the Eucharist and from prayer, because they confess not the Eucharist to be the flesh of our Saviour Jesus Christ, which suffered for our sins and which the Father of His goodness, raised up again. Those, therefore, who speak against this gift of God, incur death in the midst of their disputes.

Recall the sentiments expressed by the disciples who left Jesus, saying the Eucharist saying (teaching) "is hard" (John 6:66). From what St. Ignatius writes, early Church members had doubts, and so do some of the faithful today. The question that helps us to solidify the truth of the Real Presence from this passage becomes: Why even bring up this topic of the unbelief of Christ's eucharistic presence if the understanding of the Church at that time was that the bread and wine were mere symbols and not the actual Body, Blood, soul, and divinity of our Lord himself? In their mention, these different opinions serve as testimony to the actual belief of the early Church in Christ's Presence in the Eucharist.

St. Ignatius' Letter to the Philadelphians 4

Take heed, then, to have but one Eucharist. For there is one flesh of Our Lord Jesus Christ, and one cup to [show forth] the unity of His blood; one altar; as there is one bishop, along with the presbytery and deacons, my fellow-servants: that so, whatsoever you do, you may do it according to [the will of] God.

While St. Ignatius' mention of the flesh and blood of Christ in the context of the Eucharist speaks for itself, we might ask what he meant by saying "have but one Eucharist."

Ignatius most likely is leveling this line at a group known as the Judaizers. They acknowledged that Jesus was the Messiah, but insisted, contrary to St. Peter's ruling at the Council of Jerusalem, that new converts to Christianity must first be circumcised. Plus, Judaizers believed the Lord's Day, and thereby the celebration of the Eucharist, should not be held on Sunday, as it had been by the Christians under St. Peter, but should remain on the Jewish Sabbath, Saturday.

Saint Ignatius argued in this writing that there can be only one, consistent, universal eucharistic celebration. Ignatius' charge for one common day of eucharistic celebration seamlessly echoes Jesus' ardent desire for the unity he expressed in his prayer to the Father:

And I have given them the glory you gave me, so that they may be one, as we are one. I in them and you in me, that they may be brought to perfection as one, that the world may know that you sent me, and that you loved them even as you loved me.

John 17:22–23

It is not surprising that these verses come from the Gospel of John. Having been a disciple of St. John, St. Ignatius insists on the same action of unity and call for oneness throughout the Church, and most especially in the Eucharist. If the Eucharist were a mere symbol, a common meal, the emphasis on a single Eucharist celebration wouldn't make sense. Neither would the insistence that it is the real flesh and blood of Christ that is being celebrated, if it were not so.

St. Ignatius' Letter to the Smyrnaeans 8:1

> You should regard the Eucharist as valid which is celebrated either by the bishop, or by someone he authorizes.

The Eucharist is held in such reverence that only an ordained bishop, or someone he delegates such as the presbyters (priests) mentioned in St. Ignatius' letter to the Philadelphians, can lead the liturgy.

This writing came fewer than ten years after the death of the last living apostle, St. John. Consider that if St. Ignatius were writing all that he did on the Eucharist in or near the year 107, it is reasonable to believe that the eucharistic practices he described had been used in the Church for some time.

Saint John stood at Jesus' side for three years, recorded in the detail of a firsthand observer the life and words of Jesus, and directly instructed St. Ignatius, who then left accounts of the Eucharist. This trail of truth is as direct as it gets, so much so that believing that the Eucharist is anything but the Real Presence of Christ becomes increasingly difficult.

We now turn our attention to the year 155 and the writings of St. Justin Martyr.

ST. JUSTIN MARTYR

Saint Justin Martyr was born in Samaria around the year 100. A learned man, Justin's initial education led him through philosophical waters that he never found satisfying. During a chance meeting with a Syrian Christian, the man shared a powerful testimony for the Christian faith with Justin, who was so moved by it that he renounced his past philosophical learnings and began serving the emerging Christian faith.

Saint Justin Martyr put his intellectual talents to work for the Church, becoming an outstanding apologist of the faith against the many heresies that confronted the second-century Church. He was so fervent a believer in Christ, he was martyred for it in 165.

In *First Apology*, a book written between 153 and 155, St. Justin Martyr provides a vivid description of the Mass of his time. What is remarkable to anyone who has attended the current Mass is how similar the Mass of Justin Martyr's time is to the Mass of today.

Because St. Justin was so detailed in his description of the Mass, I will break his writing into three components from chapters 65–67. My first two divisions should sound familiar to the Catholic reader, as they are similar in their content to the two distinct components of the current Mass: the Liturgy of the Word and the Liturgy of the Eucharist. The third and final section of St. Justin Martyr's writings includes general commentary on the Eucharist.

THE LITURGY OF THE WORD, CHAPTERS 65 AND 67

...Those who are called brethren are assembled in order that we may offer hearty prayers in common for ourselves and for the baptized [illuminated] person, and for all others in every place, that we may be counted worthy, now that we have learned the truth, by our works also to be found good citizens and keepers of the commandments, so that we may be saved with an everlasting salvation. Having ended the prayers, we salute one another with a kiss. There is then brought to the president of the brethren bread and a cup of wine mixed with water; and he taking them gives praise and glory to the Father of the universe....

First Apology, chapter 65

And on the day called Sunday, all who live in cities or in the country gather together in one place, and the memoirs of the apostles or the writings of the prophets are read, as long as time permits; then, when the reading has ceased, the president verbally instructs, and exhorts the imitation of these good things. Then we all rise together and pray, and, as we before said, when our prayer is ended, bread and wine and water are brought...there is distribution to each and a participation of that over which thanks has been given, and to those who are absent a portion is sent by the deacons. And they who are well to do and willing, give what each thinks fit; and what is collected is deposited with the president, who succors the orphans and widows and those who, through sickness or any other cause or want, and those who are in bonds and the strangers sojourning among use, and in a word takes care of all who are in need.

First Apology, chapter 67

As is the case today, Justin's Sunday Mass begins with prayers and readings. Of particular interest are the types of readings identified: writings from the apostles and the prophets. Like at today's Mass, the first reading is from the Old Testament, the second from the New Testament. The prophets of St. Justin's Mass correspond to our reading of the Old Testament. Similarly, Justin's memoirs of the apostles parallel our present reading of the New Testament and/or Gospels. After these readings, the president, known today as the presider or celebrant, then speaks to the congregation, urging them to follow the good things from the readings. Known today as the homily, it occurs at the same point in the Mass as it did in Justin's time, immediately following the Scripture readings.

Saint Justin also details the sharing of common prayers. Included therein is what the Church today calls the Penitential Act. This prayer is where those assembled admit their faults and seek God's forgiveness of their minor transgressions in order to worthily receive the Body and Blood of Christ. Saint Justin Martyr was referring to this when he says we may be counted worthy. When the prayers end, the congregation greets one another with a kiss. Although it now takes place in the Liturgy of the Eucharist, this action, known as the sign of peace, still continues to be celebrated in Mass today.

In what we today call the offertory, St. Justin brings up both current components of this part of the Mass: the presentation of the gifts of bread and wine, and a financial collection to support those in need. He also mentions that a little water is mixed in with the wine to commemorate not only the blood that was shed by Christ, but also the water that poured from his lanced side. Just as it was done in the Mass of the year 155, the same mingling of water and the wine occurs in the Mass of today, performed by either the priest or deacon. Today, and most likely then, the water represents Christ's humanity and the wine his divinity. Thus, we receive the Body, Blood, soul, and divinity of Christ in a real way in the Eucharist.

ADMINISTRATION
OF THE SACRAMENTS, CHAPTER 65

...There is then brought to the president of the brethren bread and a cup of wine mixed with water; and he taking them, gives praise and glory to the Father of the universe, through the name of the Son and of the Holy Spirit, and offers thanks at considerable length for our being counted worthy to receive these things at His hands. And when he has concluded the prayers and thanksgiving, all the people present express their assent by saying Amen....and when the president has given thanks, and all the people have expressed their assent, those who are called by us deacons give to each of those present to partake of the bread and wine mixed with water over which the thanksgiving was pronounced, and to those who are absent, they carry away a portion.

First Apology, chapter 65

The president, presider, or celebrant of the Mass is either a bishop or priest. After receiving the gifts of bread and wine, the president "gives praise and glory...and offers thanks at considerable length." Once again, this is exactly what happens in the Mass today. It is during these prayers where the bread and wine are transformed into the Body, Blood, soul, and divinity of our Lord, Jesus Christ. Another modern-day similarity between the Mass from thousands of years ago and the Mass offered today is the individual response to the eucharistic gifts. Then, as now, we say "Amen" when offered this most holy and sacred gift.

ADMINISTRATION
OF THE EUCHARIST, CHAPTER 66

In this chapter, St. Justin offers a deeper statement of faith as it pertains to the Real Presence of Christ in the Eucharist. Coming immediately after the description of the Liturgy of the Eucharist, St. Justin Martyr explains more about the Eucharist just received:

> And this food is called among us Εὐχαριστία [the Eucharist], of which no one is allowed to partake but the man who believes that the things which we teach are true, and who has been washed with the washing that is for the remission of sins, and unto regeneration, and who is so living as Christ has enjoined. For not as common bread and common drink do we receive these; but in like manner as Jesus Christ our Saviour, having been made flesh by the Word of God, had both flesh and blood for our salvation, so likewise have we been taught that the food which is blessed by the prayer of His word, and from which our blood and flesh by transmutation are nourished, is the flesh and

blood of that Jesus who was made flesh. For the apostles, in the memoirs composed by them, which are called Gospels, have thus delivered unto us what was enjoined upon them; that Jesus took bread, and when He had given thanks, said, This do in remembrance of Me, Luke 22:19 this is My body; and that, after the same manner, having taken the cup and given thanks, He said, This is My blood; and gave it to them....

First Apology, chapter 66

While this whole section is laced in eucharistic proof of the Real Presence, St. Justin's comments with this quote resonate with particular clarity. In his use of the word *transmutation*, St. Justin Martyr could not be any clearer in his juxtaposition of these two lines that this Bread of Life is anything but common. Rather it has been transformed through prayerful consecration into the flesh and blood of the incarnate Jesus.

The continuity St. Justin lays out looks similar to our eucharistic relay analogy. In chapter 66, he traces the early Church's understanding of the Eucharist back to the source, Jesus, then through his apostles, and then to himself as a Father of the Church. All this happened in a little more than 100 years. The chance is slim that the teaching of the Real Presence of the Eucharist had become distorted by the time of St. Justin. When we add this to the writings of the apostles and St. Ignatius—coupled with the *Didache*—there lies little room for doubt about the accurate transmission of Jesus' teaching to this period of time.

Now, let's move to the mid-third century and the writings of St. Irenaeus.

ST. IRENAEUS

Saint Irenaeus was born in Smyrna in the year 130. Like St. Ignatius, St. Irenaeus has a connection to St. John the Apostle, as he was a student of St. Polycarp, who himself was a disciple of St. John. Irenaeus was a Greek bishop whose most famous writing, *Against Heresies*, contains five books and was written between 180 and 190. Saint Irenaeus is the first to mention the action and perhaps the moment when the bread and wine become the Eucharist:

> He has declared the cup, a part of creation, to be his own blood, from which he causes our blood to flow; and the bread, a part of creation, he has established as his own body, from which he gives increase unto our bodies. When, therefore, the mixed cup [wine and water] and the baked bread receives the Word of God and becomes the Eucharist, the body of Christ, and from these the substance of our flesh is increased and supported, how can they say that the flesh is not capable of receiving the gift of God, which is eternal

life—flesh which is nourished by the body and blood
of the Lord, and is in fact a member of him?

Against Heresies, Book V, verses 2–3

Known today as the institution narrative or consecration, at
the moment during the Mass when the priest holds both his
hands over the bread and wine and invokes the Holy Spirit,
the power of the words and actions of Christ and the power of
the Holy Spirit make sacramentally present under the species
of bread and wine Christ's Body and Blood. Saint Irenaeus'
words are the earliest reference to anything coming close to
the transubstantiation referred to today.

Whether the early Church considered those words as the
moment of epiclesis or not, what is clear from the writings of
St. Irenaeus is that there can be no doubt that the Christian
Church of the second century, like that of the first century,
believed that the substance of bread and wine had indeed
been transformed into the Real Presence of Christ.

We look now at another early Church Father who wrote
during the same period as St. Irenaeus, Origen of Alexandria.

ORIGEN OF ALEXANDRIA

Origen of Alexandria was born in year 184 into a devout Christian family. His father was martyred for his belief in Christ
when Origen was quite young. This loss left a deep mark upon
Origen and helped to lead him toward a life of asceticism and

a deep analysis of Scripture. Among other accomplishments, Origen put together the first translation and commentary of the Hebrew Bible. He also wrote hundreds of homilies covering almost the entire Bible. Origen is universally regarded as one of most influential people in early Christian theology.

Of interest to us are Origen's comments on the Eucharist found in his homilies on Exodus 13:3: "You are accustomed to take in the divine mysteries, so know how, when you have received the Body of the Lord, you reverently exercise every care lest a particle of it fall, and lest anything of the consecrated gift perish..." (*Homilies on Exodus* [after year 244]).

The Church teaches that every piece of the consecrated host (the Bread of Life) contains the fullness of God's Presence. Out of the same concern Origen expressed, great care is exercised today in the distribution of holy Communion. As an example, at one Sunday Mass, I noticed that as I lifted a host from the ciborium that a small particle of the Eucharist fell from my thumb to the kneeler in front me. After putting a hand of caution out to the communicant who was about to kneel to receive the Eucharist, I looked at the kneeler and spotted the particle of the host (Christ). I bent over, pressed my finger on the particle, and placed it on my tongue. The reason is twofold. First, knowing that every fragment of the eucharistic host is Christ, it is inappropriate to knowingly allow our Lord to be knelt on or stepped on. Second, relating to our previous discussion of the Passover, all of the lamb of the Old and New Covenants must be consumed.

This is also the reason that at Mass you will see the priest and deacon take great care in purifying the sacred vessels after the distribution of holy Communion. When water is poured into a used, seemingly empty ciborium, the water quickly alights with a multitude of eucharistic particles. The clergy member then, out of reverence for the Blessed Sacrament, ingests the water and accompanying fragments.

Based on Origen's comment, it appears this same degree of reverence for every fragment of the Eucharist was in place in the early Church. If the Eucharist were merely bread (a symbol), would such reverence have been observed?

ST. CYRIL OF JERUSALEM

Moving to the mid-fourth century, we turn to the last Church Father to discuss, St. Cyril of Jerusalem. Born in 315, St. Cyril, was learned. He is one of just thirty-six doctors of the Church. Cyril is best known for his writings on the instruction of catechumens (those new to the faith) and on the order of the holy liturgy during his time. He also is recognized for making Jerusalem a central place of pilgrimage for Christians.

Among his many writings are several that directly address the question of the Real Presence of Christ in the Eucharist. Based on the content of the next two quotations from St. Cyril in the year 350, it appears the Church of the fourth century held firm to Jesus' original teaching.

Catechetical Lectures 19:7: "For as the Bread and Wine of the Eucharist before the invocation of the Holy and Adorable Trinity were simple bread and wine, while after the invocation the bread becomes the body of Christ, and the wine the blood of Christ." Cyril is describing transubstantiation, the miracle by which bread and wine become, through the invocation of the Holy Trinity, the completeness of Christ himself.

Catechetical Lectures 22:6: In this writing, Cyril dovetails the reality of transubstantiation to describe its human ramification on the faithful. "Contemplate, therefore, the bread and wine not as bare elements, for they are, according to the Lord's declaration, the body and blood of Christ; for though sense suggests this to thee, let faith establish thee. Judge not the matter from taste, but from faith be fully assured without misgiving, that thou hast been vouchsafed the body and blood of Christ."

In short, St. Cyril is saying that although the matter presented looks, smells, and tastes like bread and wine, it is not. Through the invocation of the priest, it is transformed into the Body and Blood of Christ. This is hard for our finite, human minds to comprehend. But as we know, all things are possible with God!

Having journeyed through the prefigurements of the Eucharist, through the teachings of Jesus, and through those same teachings being gracefully echoed by both the apostles and the early Church Fathers, the "heavy lifting" is complete.

I use that term because many are aware or have access to the teachings of the Church today. Much harder is traversing down the long hallway of history to look for connections to the present. My hope is that your belief in the Eucharist has been sparked or deepened. At the least, I hope you are considering my points.

With three successful handoffs of the baton now complete, each revealing a remarkable consistency in teaching through time, we now turn to the final leg of our eucharistic relay, the teachings of the Church today.

CHAPTER 7

Leg Four:
The Teachings
of the Church Today

This chapter will be shorter than the others because I have completed the "heavy lifting" of chronicling the past and because the Church's understanding and teaching about the Eucharist has changed little in more than 2,000 years.

While we may have more elegant, intellectual, and perhaps more poetic ways of describing our understanding of this superlative gift of grace, the core teaching and understanding of the Eucharist has remained the same since the inception of the Eucharist.

This strengthens my belief. This is what morphs my thick Thomaslike disposition to more resemble the heart of a receptive child. There has not been a single alteration in this teaching since Jesus himself shared it with his disciples. The baton has not dropped once. No runner of this race of truth has come close to committing a lane violation. In addition, we should consider the abundant mention of this Bread of Heaven long before it even existed.

It started with the Book of Genesis and the gifts of Melchizedek, the king of Jerusalem. The seismic reverberation of this early concept continued with the foreshadowing of the Passover, to the manna of the Exodus, and into and through the sacred Bread of Presence. From the beginning, God's earth echoed with this promise of grace, a promise realized through Christ himself at the Last Supper and reverently carried forward to this day.

Sadly, misunderstanding and heresy about the Eucharist is part of its history and exists today. Thankfully, whenever such a heresy presented itself throughout history, it was quickly responded to, first by the apostles, then by the Church Fathers, and throughout the span of Church leadership to this day. The consistency of such response serves as a witness to its very Truth.

As stated in the song "Once in a Lifetime" by the band the Talking Heads, "Same as it ever was; same as it ever was" is my understanding of the Blessed Sacrament from Jesus to today. Nothing has changed since its inception by Jesus to this moment in time. This chapter wraps with some quotes from the *Catechism* on who and what the Eucharist is. If, after reading the previous chapter, if it all sounds pretty familiar to you, remember: "Same as it ever was; same as it ever was."

THE SPIRITUAL GOOD OF THE CHURCH

The Eucharist is the source and summit of the Christian life. The other sacraments, and indeed all ecclesiastical ministries and works of the apostolate, are bound up with the Eucharist and are oriented toward it. For in the Blessed Eucharist is contained the whole spiritual good of the Church, namely Christ himself, our Pasch.

CCC 1324

In the most Blessed Sacrament of the Eucharist "the body and blood, together with the soul and divinity, of our Lord Jesus Christ and, therefore, the whole Christ is truly, really, and substantially contained." This presence is called "real"—by which is not intended to exclude the other types of Presence as if they could not be "real" too, but because it is Presence in the fullest sense: that is to say, it is a substantial Presence by which Christ, God, and man, makes himself wholly and entirely Present.

CCC 1374

If it sounds like I am being repetitious, I am. Yes, early in the book some of these same quotes from the *Catechism* were discussed. But I'm not just creating a *deja-vu* echo chamber. Your familiarity with the contents from these two paragraphs is likely due more to a component of the consistency involved in the eucharistic narrative.

As it has been taught from the start, "the whole Christ is truly, really, substantially contained" in the Eucharist. The Eucharist is the "source and the summit" of the Christian life because it is Christ, God, and man made wholly and entirely present to us. The Eucharist contains the whole spiritual good of the Church because it is the whole of our faith, it is Jesus Christ! It is our spiritual summit because of what it is, not what it represents, and because of what it gives: grace in its most abundant form.

MODERN-DAY SAINTS ON THE EUCHARIST

We finish leg four of our relay with some beautiful eucharistic quotes from a select few modern-day saints and/or saints-to-be. As was with the quotes from the *Catechism*, there is nothing new, theologically speaking, to report to you. Rather, they are presented without commentary for you to soak in, meditate upon, and help you to deepen your faith in the Real Presence of the Eucharist. As you read them, look for their consistent beauty, truth, and gifts of grace.

Saint Maria Faustina Kowalska (1905–38)
"Holy Communion assures me that I will win the victory; and so, it is. I fear the day when I do not receive holy Communion. This bread of the Strong gives me all the strength I need to carry on my mission and to do whatever the Lord asks of me."

Saint John Paul II (1920–2005)
In his encyclical letter On the Eucharist and its Relationship to the Church *(Ecclesia de Eucharistia):* "For the most holy Eucharist contains the Church's entire spiritual wealth: Christ himself, our Passover and living bread. Through his own flesh, now made living and life-giving by the Holy Spirit, he offers life to men."

Venerable Archbishop Fulton J. Sheen (1895–1979)
"The greatest love story of all time is...in a tiny white Host."

Saint Padre Pio (1887–1968)
"If we only knew how God regards this Sacrifice, we would risk our lives to be present at a single Mass."

Saint Teresa of Calcutta (1910–97)
"Jesus has made Himself the Bread of Life to give us life. Night and day, He is there. If you really want to grow in love, come back to the Eucharist, come back to that Adoration.

"Nowhere on Earth are we more welcomed or loved than by Jesus in Eucharist."

POST-RACE REFLECTIONS

As *For Real?* nears its conclusion, I am reevaluating my initial motives for writing it. Did I write it for the Catholics who Pew Research found do not believe in the Real Presence? Did I write it for evangelicals who believe their Communion service (as well as our own Catholic Mass) is just a symbol? Did I write it for Catholics who want to deepen their understanding of this extraordinary gift? Yes, yes, and yes.

But I also wonder if another motive was involved, a selfish one, that might help me atone for my period of doubt. Something that might expiate me from my misguided instruction to my children. Or perhaps the reason I wrote it might be found in my self-centered hopes of trading in some of my Thomaslike tendencies for the pure, believing heart of a child. Confronted with this, I once again answer: yes, yes, and yes.

Motivation aside, the facts remain. Evangelical Protestants believe the Eucharist is nothing more than a symbol. A report says two-thirds of people who call themselves Catholic do not believe in the Real Presence of Christ in the Eucharist. Most notable is that, of Catholics who attend Mass regularly, still one-third may also fall into the category of nonbelief.

Believers may not understand, but a subset of childlike hearts don't need apologetics and reasoning to believe. I wish I were one of them. Perhaps because I'm not one of them I understand there are likely more Thomaslike individuals who will benefit from explanations than those who won't.

All the same, I hope that regardless of where your beliefs lie, God has graced you with a movement of heart. I hope you have made steps to either change or deepen your beliefs.

While I've shared a lot of historical facts and faith-filled beliefs in the hopes of drawing both you and me deeper into the beautiful mystery of the Eucharist, I want to end my formal commentary by revisiting the benefit of the Eucharist: the overabundant outpouring of God's grace.

Recall that the Church's definition of grace has three parts. First is that we do not deserve it, yet God gives it. Second, grace increases within us the ability to both hear and then respond to his call, a call he never ceases to send. And third, our response leads us to become his adoptive children, partakers in his divine nature.

The Eucharist is the source and summit of our faith because Christ is the source, he is the Eucharist. And within the Eucharist comes so much grace, so much power to answer his call with a resounding yes and to draw ever nearer to him. God's grace cannot be given in any greater portion than in the Eucharist. There are other ways to obtain grace, but knowing this about the Eucharist, knowing the rich abundance that resides in it, in him, why would—how could—anyone say no?

We can be no nearer to God now than when we receive his completeness, his Body, Blood, soul, and divinity—in the Eucharist. God knew this and therefore gave us this unimaginable gift.

CHAPTER 8

Evangelizing the Eucharist: Sharing the Truth of the Real Presence

I n section 14 of his encyclical on Evangelization in the Modern World *(Evangelii Nuntiandi)*, St. Paul VI famously wrote, "She [the Church] exists to evangelize." Later in that same document, St. Paul VI raises those stakes in what I consider to be the quintessential line regarding the faithful's call to evangelize:

> Finally, the person who has been evangelized goes on to evangelize others. Here lies the test of Truth, the touchstone of evangelization: it is unthinkable that a person should accept the Word and give himself to the kingdom without becoming a person who bears witness to it and proclaims it in his turn.
>
> *Evangelii Nuntiandi* 24

As members of the Church, we have a responsibility to share the truth of our faith to others. This is scary for many. Most often, this fear is generated by a misunderstanding of what it means to evangelize. When many hear the word *evangelize*, they picture a guy wearing a sandwich board with "Repent" written in thick, bold red paint on one side, and John 3:16 on the other. In the mind of the fearful, this figment of false evangelization is also waving a Bible in one hand while quoting Bible verses through a bullhorn. If this is what it means to evangelize, I would want no part of it, either!

Many components make up what it means to evangelize and how best to do so. For our purposes, know two things:

- Being a member of the Catholic Church, we have a duty to pass on what we ourselves hold dear and know to be true.
- While sharing our faith takes on different forms and methods, there will come a time when you will be asked a question regarding your faith. Or if not a direct question, an opportunity will likely present itself where you will feel the tug of the Holy Spirit asking you to provide comment regarding your faith to another.

It stands to reason that the Eucharist, specifically Christ's Real Presence, is a natural topic for questions. Just glance again at the Pew Research data and realize how much doubt exists about this lofty matter. I hope every Catholic who believes in the Real Presence is prepared to explain his or her belief, giving sound reasoning and proactively seeking opportunities to share this critical belief with others.

Responding to a question on the Eucharist can be difficult, but I have a suggestion, a method, on how to get the main points of what's been presented here across in a direct, condensed, and easy-to-remember way.

SHARING THE EUCHARISTIC TRUTH WITH OTHERS

Remember three key points to help you pass on the truth of Real Presence effectively:

Key 1: These eucharistic truths are an unchanged continuum of teaching that began with Jesus. Falsely purported to be an invention of the fourth-century Church, Jesus announced the Real Presence of the Eucharist, and that teaching—his teaching—has never been altered by the Catholic Church.

Key 2: Remember that a relay race has four components. This offers a memorable framework from which to transmit this teaching model. The relay metaphor serves as a reminder to touch on not only the four periods of time discussed in the book (the Teachings of Jesus, the Teachings of the Apostles, the Teaching of the early Church Fathers, the Teachings of the Church Today), but also to accentuate the seamless handoff from one to the next ("same as it ever was").

Key 3: Add meat to the bones of that framework. That is, state one or two facts from each "relay heat" to convey the core teachings of each period of time and each relay leg.

Below is a sample dialog on how presenting the relay race analogy might go. It is not a script, nor the only way to introduce and discuss the topic. It serves as a thought starter. Notice keys 1 and 2 are used in the introductory comments to help establish the facts that follow. Likewise, notice when you get to each of the four relay legs that key 3, the delivery of one or two convincing facts or in-depth components, is used. A less-detailed guide as an example to the relay-race analogy follows this sample response.

SAMPLE RESPONSE (DETAILED)

General Introduction

The main intellectual reason I believe the Eucharist is the Real Presence of Christ is based on the teachings of Jesus himself. When you look into what Jesus taught about the Eucharist, it is difficult to come away with any other understanding. What strengthens my belief is how these teachings moved forward, in an unbroken chain—unchanged, and with amazing consistency—from Jesus to the Twelve Apostles, through the early Church, and into today.

Introduction of the Relay Race

To give you specifics on the consistency of eucharistic teaching, I will use the analogy of a successful four-by-four relay race.

The first leg of the race begins with the teachings of Jesus on the Eucharist. Jesus then hands off the relay baton to leg two of the relay, the apostles. The apostles then hand the baton—the teachings on the Eucharist that started with Jesus—to those in authority who immediately followed them: the Church Fathers. Finally, the Church Fathers hand on these teachings of the Eucharist to all who follow after them, including the Church of today.

Again, the amazing thing is that when we look into what is taught within each of these four relay segments, we discover a wonderful uniformity in teaching. The teaching of Jesus on the Eucharist is exactly what the Church has believed and taught within the Church from year 33 to this day.

Here is what the historical record says about each of these relay segments. We start with the most important "racer" in this equation, what Jesus himself taught about the Eucharist.

Leg One: The Teachings of Jesus

- His most specific teaching on the Eucharist comes from the Gospel of John 6 in what is known as the Bread of Life Discourse.
- More than 5,000 people attended and heard Jesus speak.
- During the discourse, Jesus said four times, using various words, "Unless you eat my flesh and drink my blood, you have no life in you."

- In John 6, the word for "to eat" is mentioned fifteen times. Generally, the Greek word for *eat* is *phago*. It is used in eleven of the fifteen references. During the four times Jesus talks about eating as it pertains to himself (as in, "eat my flesh") he uses the word *trogon,* which means to gnaw, crunch, or chew. Trogon is used only six times in the entire Bible. It is plain to see from its usage that Jesus was not speaking symbolically of eating his flesh, but rather literally.

- At the end of the discourse, "many" disciples (scholars believe "many" represents thousands of disciples) approached Jesus and said, "This saying (teaching) is hard." Then these disciples, many of whom had dropped everything to follow Jesus, turned and left him. If Jesus was speaking metaphorically, why did he not stop those individuals, who loved and adored him, to explain that he was speaking symbolically? The answer is simple: he meant every word he said.

Leg Two: The Teachings of the Apostles

- As in a relay, Jesus' teachings on the Eucharist are handed off directly to the apostles. In studying the writings of the New Testament, we find that Jesus' Real Presence in the Eucharist is taught by those who followed him.

- More than 125 New Testament verses link to the Eucharist. Saint Paul, one of the greatest and most influential of all the apostles, writes directly about the Eucharist in his letter of instruction to the Church in Corinth. Paul writes that at the Last Supper, Jesus said, "This is my body, this is my blood." He later goes on to warn the Church of Corinth about receiving the Eucharist unworthily, that is in a state of sin, stating that if they do so, they cast judgment on themselves. If the bread and wine were mere symbols, how could anyone be unworthy to receive the components of a common, ordinary meal?

- First Corinthians was written between the years 53 and 54, shortly after Jesus' death and resurrection, illustrating that the teaching of the Real Presence was recognized and taught in the early Church.

Leg Three: The Teaching of the Early Church Fathers

The next question is, were these same teachings and understandings of the Eucharist received and taught by those in authority in the Church after the apostles? To answer that, we turn to the third leg of the relay and look at the writings of the early Church Fathers, those who followed immediately after the apostles:

- While hundreds of quotes and writings from the Church Fathers support the consistent belief in the Real Presence of the Eucharist, one of the most pertinent is from St. Ignatius of Antioch. He is critically relevant not only because of the early date of his writing, year 107, soon after the death of the Apostle John, but also because St. Ignatius was a disciple of John the Apostle.

- "What I want is God's bread," Ignatius writes, "which is the flesh of Christ, who came from David's line, and for drink I want his blood: an immortal feast indeed!" In another one of his writings, St. Ignatius speaks about some people of that time who do not believe in Christ's Real Presence in the Eucharist. This controversy proves the early Church did indeed believe in Christ's eucharistic presence.

Leg Four: The Teaching of the Church Today

Finally, having its origins in Jesus himself, the belief and teaching in the Real Presence of the Eucharist has traveled seamlessly and without change from the apostles, through the Church Fathers, to the final relay leg, the Church today.

- So much has been written about this within the last century that there can be no denial, by believer or nonbeliever, that the Catholic Church of today teaches and affirms that the Eucharist is indeed the Body and Blood of Christ.
- The *Catechism* affirms: In the Blessed Sacrament of the Eucharist "the body and blood, together with the soul and divinity, of our Lord Jesus Christ and, therefore, the whole Christ is truly, really, and substantially contained (*CCC* 1374).

SAMPLE RESPONSE (SIMPLIFIED)

To further simplify the eucharistic relay presentation, it is outlined here with a few key words:

THE EUCHARISTIC RELAY

Like a successful relay race, the teachings of the Real Presence of Christ in the Eucharist have been handed off from Jesus, without fault, change, or adjustment from the time of Christ to today.

LEG ONE:
THE TEACHINGS OF JESUS

- John 6: The Bread of Life Discourse
- More than 5,000 in attendance.
- Jesus says "unless you eat my flesh" four times. For the word *eat* when referencing himself, he uses *trogon*, which means "to gnaw or chew."
- Many disciples left Jesus due to this teaching. Notice Jesus did not stop them to explain he was speaking symbolically because he wasn't.

LEG TWO:
THE TEACHINGS OF THE APOSTLES

- The New Testament contains more than 125 verses linked to the Eucharist.
- Saint Paul writes about eating the bread and drinking the cup in 1 Corinthians.
- First Corinthians was written only eleven years after Jesus left earth.

LEG THREE:
THE EARLY CHURCH FATHERS

- Hundreds of quotes and writings from the Church Fathers support the consistent belief in the Real Presence of Christ in the Eucharist.
- Saint Ignatius, a disciple of John the Apostle, writes in year 107, shortly after the death of John, that he wants God's bread, which is the flesh of Christ, and his blood for drink.

LEG FOUR:
THE CHURCH TODAY

- Over the last century, a multitude of writings and formal teachings have been added to the public record to demonstrate what the Catholic Church believes and promulgates: "the body and blood, together with the soul and divinity, of our Lord Jesus Christ and, *therefore the whole Christ is truly, really, and substantially contained.*" This presence is called "real" (*CCC* 1374).

About the Author: Deacon Dennis Lambert and his wife, Debbie, live in Phoenix, where he serves as a deacon in the Diocese of Phoenix. In addition to his work with the Church, Deacon Dennis writes fiction and nonfiction. His first novel, *The Table*, won two Catholic Press Association awards. In addition to his passion for writing, Deacon Dennis and Debbie share a deep love of music and have performed together in choirs and bands for almost three decades.

If you or your group are interested in the topic of this book and would like to invite Deacon Dennis to speak at your parish, conference, or special event, please contact him at deacondennislambert@gmail.com or through his website, dennislambert-writer.com.